Ready N

for use with

Financial Accounting

Second Edition

Robert Libby
Cornell University

Patricia A. Libby
Ithaca College

Daniel G. Short
Miami University

Prepared by
Jon A. Booker
Tennessee Technological University

Charles W. Caldwell
Tennessee Technological University

Susan C. Galbreath
Tennessee Technological University

Richard S. Rand
Tennessee Technological University

Boston Burr Ridge, IL Dubuque, IA Madison, WI New York San Francisco St. Louis
Bangkok Bogotá Caracas Lisbon London Madrid
Mexico City Milan New Delhi Seoul Singapore Sydney Taipei Toronto

Irwin/McGraw-Hill

*A Division of The **McGraw-Hill** Companies*

Ready Notes for use with
FINANCIAL ACCOUNTING

Previous edition 1996 by Richard D. Irwin, a Times Mirror Higher Education company.
Printed in the United States of America.

2 3 4 5 6 7 8 9 0 BBC/BBC 9 0 9 8

ISBN 0-256-25435-4

http://www.mhhe.com

Welcome to

READY NOTES

Your life just got easier! This booklet includes *Ready Notes* to accompany your textbook. *Ready Notes* were designed as a classroom supplement to accompany *Ready Shows*. More importantly, *Ready Notes* were developed for you, the student.

Somewhere in your educational experience, you have undoubtedly encountered a common dilemma facing many students; the feeling of helplessness that comes from trying to write down everything your instructor says and, at the same time, actually paying attention to what is being taught. *Ready Notes* addresses this problem by providing pre-prepared lecture outlines to accompany the *Ready Shows* your instructor will be using in class. Rather than spending time copying material that is already in the book, you will be able to focus on the most important aspects of what your instructor is actually saying. You will still be expected to take notes, but the nature of those notes will change.

Each page in *Ready Notes* includes reproductions of some of the actual projected screens that you will be seeing in class. The *Ready Notes* booklet includes the information for many of the examples that your instructor will be presenting.

It is your responsibility to attend class regularly and to be prepared for class. However, used properly, Ready Notes will help you to achieve your goals for the course. Good luck and good accounting!

CONTENTS

1. Financial Statements and Business Decisions 1-1

2. Investing and Financing Decisions and the Balance Sheet 2-1

3. Operating Decisions and the Income Statement 3-1

4. The Adjustment Process and Financial Statements 4-1

5. The Communication of Accounting Information 5-1

6. Reporting and Interpreting Sales Revenue, Receivables, and Cash 6-1

7. Reporting and Interpreting Cost of Goods Sold and Inventory 7-1

8. Reporting and Interpreting Property, Plant, and Equipment; Natural Resources; and Intangibles 8-1

9. Reporting and Interpreting Liabilities 9-1

10. Reporting and Interpreting Bonds 10-1

11. Reporting and Interpreting Owners' Equity 11-1

12. Reporting and Interpreting Investments in Other Corporations 12-1

13. Statement of Cash Flows 13-1

14. Analyzing Financial Statements 14-1

FINANCIAL ACCOUNTING

Robert Libby
Patricia Libby
Daniel Short

1

FINANCIAL STATEMENTS AND BUSINESS DECISIONS

The Objectives of Financial Accounting

Financial statements are the primary means of communicating financial information to parties outside the business organization.

Balance Sheet
Income Statement
Stakeholders

Business Background

Business owners (called investors or stockholders) look for two sources of possible gain:

Sell ownership interest in the future for more than they paid.

Receive a portion of the company's earnings in cash (dividends).

Business Background

Creditors lend money to a company for a specific length of time and gain by charging interest on the money loaned.

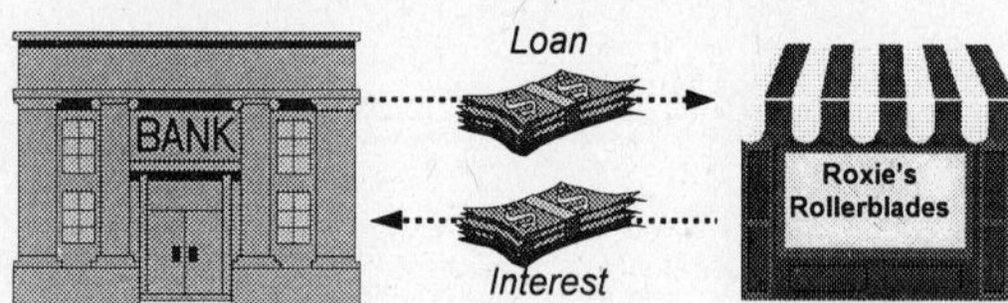

Irwin/McGraw-Hill

© The McGraw-Hill Companies, Inc., 1998

Understanding Business Operations

Manufacturers either make the parts needed to produce its products or buy the parts from suppliers.

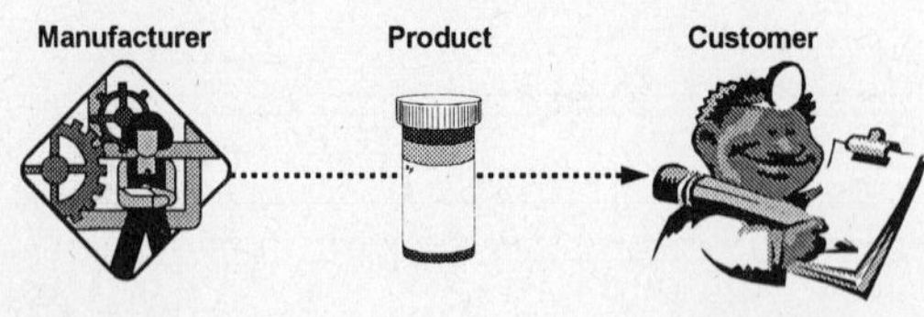

Irwin/McGraw-Hill

© The McGraw-Hill Companies, Inc., 1998

Understanding Business Operations

All businesses have an accounting system that . . .

Collects and processes financial information about an organization.

Understanding Business Operations

All businesses have an accounting system that . . .

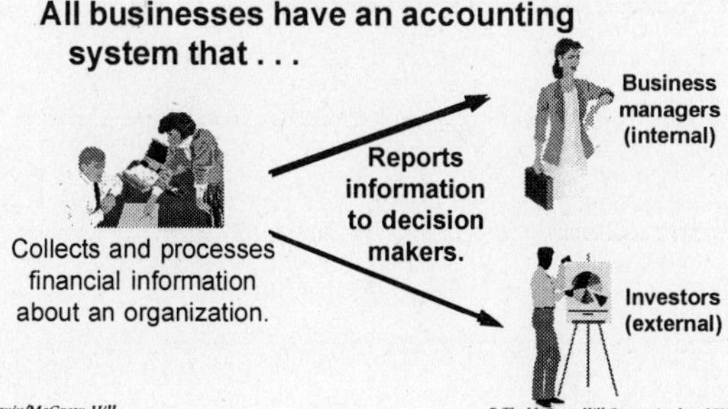

Collects and processes financial information about an organization.

Irwin/McGraw-Hill

© The McGraw-Hill Companies, Inc., 1998

Understanding Business Operations

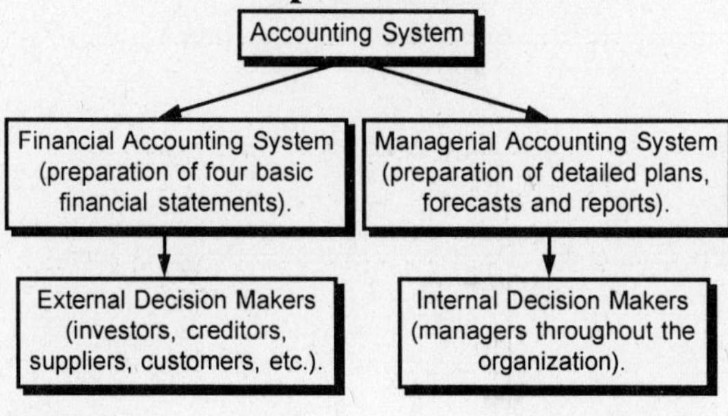

Irwin/McGraw-Hill

© The McGraw-Hill Companies, Inc., 1998

Reflecting Business Operations in Financial Statements

The four basic financial statements . . .

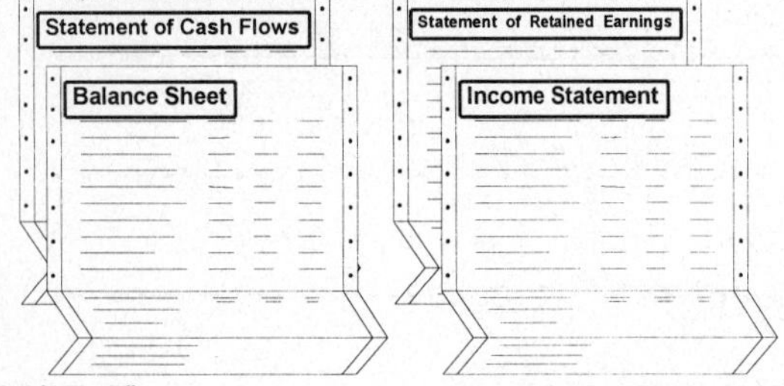

Irwin/McGraw-Hill

Reflecting Business Operations in Financial Statements

Most companies prepare financial statements at the end of the quarter (called quarterly reports) and the end of the year (called annual reports).

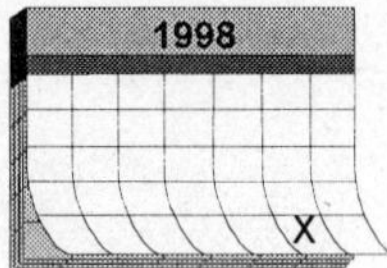

Irwin/McGraw-Hill

The Balance Sheet Heading

MAXIDRIVE CORP.
Balance Sheet
at December 31, 1998
(in thousands of dollars)

1. Name of entity (the separate-entity assumption)
2. Title of statement
3. Specific date (financial snapshot at a specific point in time)
4. Unit measure (thousands of dollars)

Irwin/McGraw-Hill

The Balance Sheet

Body of the Statement

Assets

- **probable future economic benefits owned by the business as a result of past transactions.**

Liabilities

- **probable debts or obligations of the business that result from past transactions and will be paid with assets or services in the future.**

Stockholders' Equity

- **the amount of financing provided by owners of the business and operations.**

The Balance Sheet

Basic Accounting Equation

Assets = Liabilities + Stockholders' Equity

Economic resources = Sources of financing . . .
Liabilities: from creditors
Equity: from stockholders.

World, Inc.
Balance Sheet
at December 31, 1998
(in thousands of dollars)

Assets		
Cash		$ 4,895
Accounts receivable		5,714
Inventories		8,517
Plant and equipment		7,154
Land		981
Total assets		$ 27,261
Total stockholders' equity		11,105
Total liabilities and stockholders' equity		$ 27,261

Accounts receivable - amounts owed by customers from prior sales.
Inventories - partial and completed but unsold product.
Plant and equipment - factories and production machinery.
Land - property on which factories are located.

World, Inc.
Balance Sheet
at December 31, 1998
(in thousands of dollars)

Accounts payable - amounts owed to suppliers for prior purchases.
Notes payable - amounts owed on written debt contracts.

Assets		
		$ 4,895
		5,714
		8,517
		7,154
		981
		$ 27,261
Liabilities		
Accounts payable	$ 7,156	
Notes payable	9,000	
Total liabilities		$ 16,156
Stockholders' Equity		
Contributed capital	$ 2,000	
Retained earnings	9,105	
Total stockholders' equity		11,105
Total liabilities and stockholders' equity		$ 27,261

World, Inc.
Balance Sheet
at December 31, 1998
(in thousands of dollars)

Contributed capital - amounts invested in the business by stockholders.
Retained earnings - past earnings **not** distributed to stockholders.

Assets		
Cash		$ 4,895
Accounts receivable		5,714
Inventories		8,517
Plant and equipment		7,154
Land		981
Stockholders' Equity		
Contributed capital	$ 2,000	
Retained earnings	9,105	
Total stockholders' equity		11,105
Total liabilities and stockholders' equity		$ 27,261

World, Inc.
Balance Sheet
at December 31, 1998
(in thousands of dollars)

Assets = Liabilities + Stockholders' Equity

Assets		
Cash		$ 4,895
Accounts receivable		5,714
Inventories		8,517
Plant and equipment		7,154
Land		981
		$ 27,261
Accounts payable	$ 7,156	
Notes payable	9,000	
Total liabilities		$ 16,156
Stockholders' Equity		
Contributed capital	$ 2,000	
Retained earnings	9,105	
Total stockholders' equity		11,105
Total liabilities and stockholders' equity		$ 27,261

World, Inc. Balance Sheet at December 31, 1998 (in thousands of dollars)		
Assets		
Cash		$ 4,895
Accounts receivable		5,714
Inventories		8,517
Plant and equipment		7,154
Land		981
Total assets		$ 27,261
	7,156	
	9,000	
		$ 16,156
Stockholders' Equity		
Contributed capital	$ 2,000	
Retained earnings	9,105	
Total stockholders' equity		11,105
Total liabilities and stockholders' equity		$ 27,261

Assets are listed by their ease of conversion into cash.

World, Inc. Balance Sheet at December 31, 1998 (in thousands of dollars)		
Assets		
Cash		$ 4,895
Accounts receivable		5,714
		8,517
		7,154
		981
		$ 27,261
Liabilities		
Accounts payable	$ 7,156	
Notes payable	9,000	
Total liabilities		$ 16,156
Stockholders' Equity		
Contributed capital	$ 2,000	
Retained earnings	9,105	
Total stockholders' equity		11,105
Total liabilities and stockholders' equity		$ 27,261

Liabilities are listed by their maturity (due date).

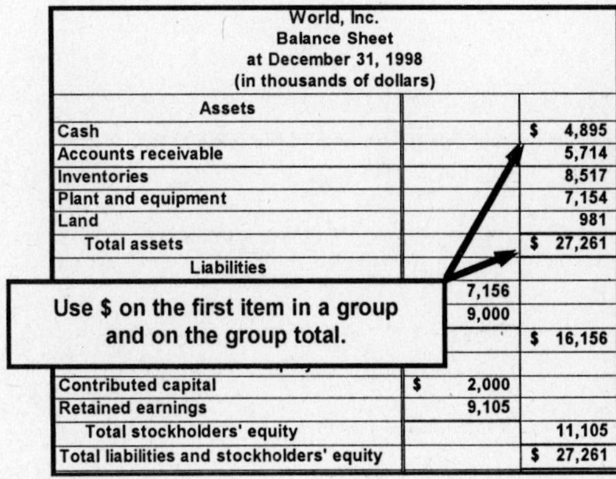

World, Inc. Balance Sheet at December 31, 1998 (in thousands of dollars)		
Assets		
Cash		$ 4,895
Accounts receivable		5,714
Inventories		8,517
Plant and equipment		7,154
Land		981
Total assets		$ 27,261
Liabilities		
	7,156	
	9,000	
		$ 16,156
Contributed capital	$ 2,000	
Retained earnings	9,105	
Total stockholders' equity		11,105
Total liabilities and stockholders' equity		$ 27,261

Use $ on the first item in a group and on the group total.

Income Statement Heading

World, Inc.
Income Statement
For the Year Ended December 31, 1998
(in thousands of dollars)

1. Name of entity
2. Title of statement
3. Specific date (Unlike the balance sheet, this statement covers a specified period of time.)
4. Unit measure (thousands of dollars)

The Income Statement

The income statement is divided into three major captions . . .

❶Revenues
❷Expenses
❸Net income

The Income Statement

❶Revenues

Earnings from the sale of goods or services.

Revenue is recognized in the period in which goods and services are sold, not necessarily the period in which cash is received.

The Income Statement

❶Revenues

Earnings from the sale of goods or services.

When will the revenue from this transaction be recognized?

$1,000 sale made on May 25th.

Cash from sale collected on June 10th.

May 1998 | June 1998

The Income Statement

❶Revenues

Earnings from the sale of goods or services.

When will the revenue from this transaction be recognized?

$1,000 revenue recognized in May

May 1998 | June 1998

The Income Statement

❷Expenses

The dollar amount of resources used up by the entity to earn revenues during a period.

An expense is recognized in the period in which goods and services are used, not necessarily the period in which cash is paid.

The Income Statement

❷Expenses

The dollar amount of resources used up by the entity to earn revenues during a period.

When will the expense for this transaction be recognized?

May 11 paid $75 cash for newspaper ad.

Ad appears on June 8th.

May 1998 | June 1998

The Income Statement

❷Expenses

The dollar amount of resources used up by the entity to earn revenues during a period.

When will the expense for this transaction be recognized?

Advertising expense recorded in June.

May 1998 | June 1998

The Income Statement

Revenues	$100
Less: Expenses	75
Net Income	$ 25

When revenues exceed expenses, we report net income.

The Income Statement

Revenues	$100
Less: Expenses	125
Net Loss	$ (25)

When expenses exceed revenues, we report net loss.

The Income Statement

Revenues	$100
Less: Expenses	100
Breakeven	$ 0

When expenses equal revenues, we operate at breakeven.

World, Inc.
Income Statement
For the Year Ended December 31, 1998
(in thousands of dollars)

Revenues		
Sales revenue		$37,436
Expenses		
Cost of goods sold	$26,980	
Selling, general and administrative	3,624	
Research and development	1,982	
Interest expense	450	
Total expenses		33,036
Pretax income		$ 4,400
Income tax expense		1,100
Net income		$ 3,300

World, Inc.
Income Statement
For the Year Ended December 31, 1998
(in thousands of dollars)

Revenues		
Sales revenue		$37,436
Expen[...]		
Cost o[...]		
Selling, general and administrative	3,624	
Research and development	1,982	
Interest expense	450	
Total expenses		33,036
Pretax income		$ 4,400
Income tax expense		1,100
Net income		$ 3,300

Sales revenue - amounts earned from the sale of goods or services during the period.

Irwin/McGraw-Hill

Cost of goods sold - the cost to produce the products sold this period.
Selling, general and administrative - operating expenses not directly related to production.
Research and development - expenses incurred to develop new products.
Interest expense - the cost of using borrowed funds.

R[...]		
S[...]		[...]$
Expenses		
Cost of goods sold	$26,980	
Selling, general and administrative	3,624	
Research and development	1,982	
Interest expense	450	
Total expenses		33,036
Pretax income		$ 4,400
Income tax expense		1,100
Net income		$ 3,300

Irwin/McGraw-Hill

World, Inc.
Income Statement
For the Year Ended December 31, 1998
(in thousands of dollars)

Revenues		
Sales revenue		$37,436
Expenses		
Cost of goods sold	$26,980	
Selling, general and administrative	3,624	
[...]		[...]6
Pretax income		$ 4,400
Income tax expense		1,100
Net income		$ 3,300

Income tax expense - income taxes on current period's pretax income.

Irwin/McGraw-Hill

Statement of Retained Earnings

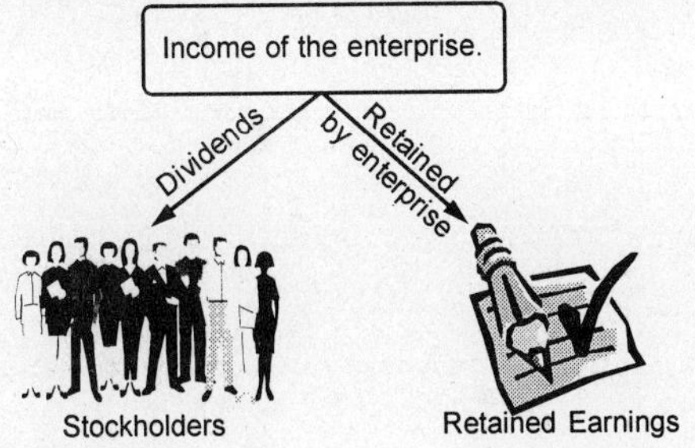

Irwin/McGraw-Hill

Statement of Retained Earnings

World, Inc.
Statement of Retained Earnings
For the Year Ended December 31, 1998
(in thousands of dollars)

Retained earnings, January 1, 1998	$ 6,805

1. Name of entity
2. Title of statement
3. Specific date (Like the income statement, this statement covers a specified period of time.)
4. Unit measure (thousands of dollars)

Irwin/McGraw-Hill

Statement of Retained Earnings

World, Inc.
Statement of Retained Earnings
For the Year Ended December 31, 1998
(in thousands of dollars)

Retained earnings, January 1, 1998	$ 6,805
Net income for 1998	3,300
Dividends for 1998	(1,000)
Retained earnings, December 31, 1998	$ 9,105

Irwin/McGraw-Hill

Statement of Cash Flows

Because revenues reported do not always equal cash collected. . .

. . . and expenses reported do not always equal cash paid . . .

Statement of Cash Flows

Because revenues reported do not always equal cash collected. . .

. . . and expenses reported do not always equal cash paid . . .

Income is usually not equal to the change in cash for the period.

World, Inc.
Statement of Cash Flows
For the Year Ended December 31, 1998
(in thousands of dollars)

Cash flows from operating activities		
Cash collected from customers	$ 33,563	
Cash paid for dividends	(1,000)	
Net cash flow from financing activities		400
Net decrease in cash during the year		$ (156)
Cash at beginning of the year		5,021
Cash at end of the year		$ 4,865

1. Name of entity
2. Title of statement
3. Specific date (Like the income statement and statement of retained earnings, this statement covers a specified period of time.)
4. Unit measure (thousands of dollars)

World, Inc.
Statement of Cash Flows
For the Year Ended December 31, 1998
(in thousands of dollars)

Cash flows from operating activities:		
Cash collected from customers	$ 33,563	
Cash paid to suppliers and employees	(30,854)	
Cash paid for interest	(450)	
Cash paid for taxes	(1,190)	
Net cash flow from operating activities		$ 1,069
Cash flow from investing activities:		
Cash paid for dividends	(1,000)	
Net cash flow from financing activities		400
Net decrease in cash during the year		$ (156)
Cash at beginning of the year		5,021
Cash at end of the year		$ 4,865

Cash flows directly related to earning income are shown in the **operating section** of the statement.

Irwin/McGraw-Hill

World, Inc.
Statement of Cash Flows
For the Year Ended December 31, 1998
(in thousands of dollars)

Cash flows from operating activities:		
	3	
	4)	
	0)	
	0)	
		$ 1,069
Cash flow from investing activities:		
Cash paid to purchase equipment	$ (1,625)	
Net cash flow from investing activities		(1,625)
Cash flow from financing activities:		
Cash received from bank loan	$ 1,400	
Cash paid for dividends	(1,000)	
Net cash flow from financing activities		400
Net decrease in cash during the year		$ (156)
Cash at beginning of the year		5,021
Cash at end of the year		$ 4,865

Cash flows related to the acquisition or sale of productive assets are shown in the **investing section** of the statement.

Irwin/McGraw-Hill

World, Inc.
Statement of Cash Flows
For the Year Ended December 31, 1998
(in thousands of dollars)

Cash flows from operating activities:		
Cash collected from customers	$ 33,563	
Cash paid to suppliers and employees	(30,854)	
Cash paid for interest	(450)	
		1,069
		(1,625)
Cash flow from financing activities:		
Cash received from bank loan	$ 1,400	
Cash paid for dividends	(1,000)	
Net cash flow from financing activities		400
Net decrease in cash during the year		$ (156)
Cash at beginning of the year		5,021
Cash at end of the year		$ 4,865

Cash flows related to the financing of the enterprise are shown in the **financing section** of the statement.

Irwin/McGraw-Hill

World, Inc. Statement of Cash Flows For the Year Ended December 31, 1998 (in thousands of dollars)		
Cash flows from operating activities:		
Cash collected from customers	$ 33,563	
Cash paid to suppliers and employees	(30,854)	
Cash paid for interest	(450)	
Cash paid for taxes	(1,190)	
Net cash flow from operating activities		$ 1,069
Cash flow from investing activities:		
Cash paid to purchase equipment	$ (1,625)	
Net cash flow from investing activities		(1,625)
Cash flow from financing activities:		
Cash received from bank loan	$ 1,400	
Cash paid for dividends	(1,000)	
Net cash flow from financing activities		400
Net decrease in cash during the year		$ (156)
Cash at beginning of the year		5,021
Cash at end of the year		$ 4,865

Notes

- ✓ Notes provide supplemental information about the financial condition of a company.
- ✓ Three types . . .
  - ❶Describe accounting rules applied.
  - ❷Present additional detail about an item on the financial statements.
  - ❸Provide additional information about an item **not** on the financial statements.

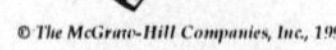

Responsibilities for the Accounting Communication Process

Effective communication means that the recipient understands what the sender intends to convey.

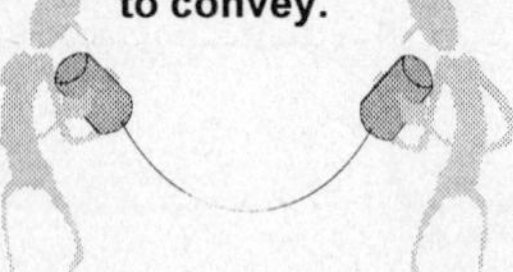

Decision makers need to understand accounting measurement rules (GAAP).

Generally Accepted Accounting Principles

Securities Act of 1933
Securities and Exchange Act of 1934

Securities and Exchange Commission (SEC) established and given broad powers to determine measurement rules for financial statements.

Generally Accepted Accounting Principles

SEC has worked closely with the accounting profession so that we could work out the detailed rules that have become known as GAAP.

Currently, the Financial Accounting Standards Board is recognized as the body to formulate GAAP.

Generally Accepted Accounting Principles

Companies are interested in GAAP because methods of reporting can have the following economic consequences . . .

1. Affect the selling price of stock.
2. Affect the amount of bonuses received by managers and other employees.
3. Cause a loss of competitive advantage.

Management Responsibility and the Demand for Auditing

Primary responsibility for the information in financial statements lies with management.

Management Responsibility and the Demand for Auditing

To ensure the accuracy of the company's records management:

- ❶ Maintains a system of controls.
- ❷ Hires an outside independent auditor.
- ❸ Board of directors review these two safeguards.

Independent Auditors

- **Auditors, generally CPAs, express an opinion as to the fairness of the financial statement presentation.**
- **Independent auditors have responsibilities that extend to the general public.**

Independent Auditors

- An audit involves . . .
  - ✓Examining the financial reports to ensure compliance with GAAP.
  - ✓Examining the underlying transactions incorporated into the financial statements.
  - ✓Expressing an opinion as to the fairness of presentation of financial information.

Irwin/McGraw-Hill

Ethics, Reputation and Legal Liability

The American Institute of Certified Public Accountants requires that all members adhere to a professional code of ethics.

Irwin/McGraw-Hill

Ethics, Reputation and Legal Liability

A CPA's reputation for honesty and competence is his/her most important asset.

Like physicians, CPAs have liability for malpractice.

Irwin/McGraw-Hill

2

INVESTING AND FINANCING DECISIONS AND THE BALANCE SHEET

Business Background

To understand amounts appearing on a company's balance sheet we need to answer these questions:

- What business activities cause changes in the balance sheet?
- How do specific activities affect each balance?
- How do companies keep track of balance sheet amounts?

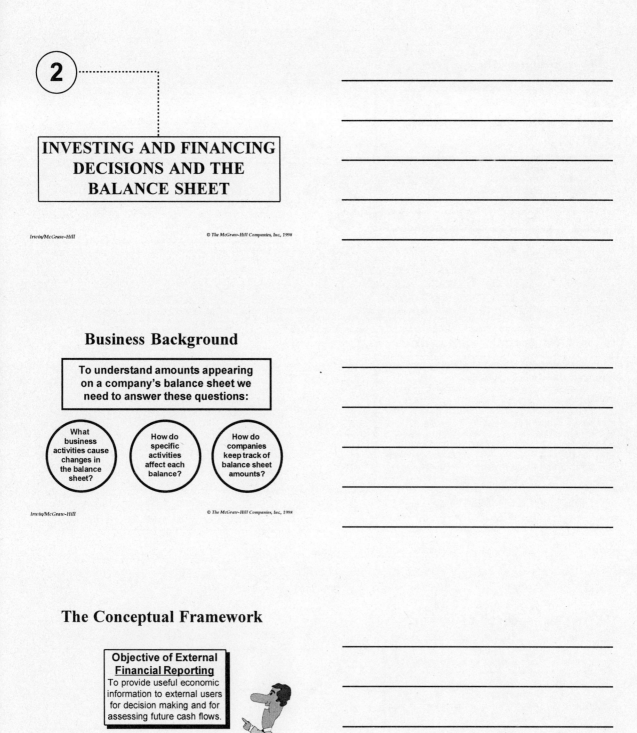

The Conceptual Framework

Objective of External Financial Reporting

To provide useful economic information to external users for decision making and for assessing future cash flows.

The Conceptual Framework

Qualitative Characteristics of Information

Overall -

Cost Benefit: Benefits of accounting and reporting should exceed cost.

Primary -

Relevance: Information must be timely and have predictive and feedback value.

Reliability: Information must be unbiased and verifiable.

Secondary -

Comparability: Information can be compared to other businesses.

Consistency: Information can be compared across time.

The Conceptual Framework

Elements of Financial Statements

Assets: Probable future economic benefits owned by the entity from past transactions.

Liabilities: Debts or obligations from past transactions to be paid with assets or services.

Stockholders' Equity: Financing provided by owners and operations.

Revenues: Inflows of net assets from ongoing operations.

Expenses: Outflows of net assets from ongoing operations.

Gains: Inflows of net assets from peripheral transactions.

Losses: Outflows of net assets from peripheral transactions.

The Conceptual Framework

Assumptions

Separate-entity: Transactions of the business are separate from transactions of owners.

Unit-of-measure: Accounting measures are in the national monetary unit ($).

Continuity: The entity will not go out of business in the near future.

Time-period: The long life of a company can be reported over a series of shorter time periods.

The Conceptual Framework

Principles

Cost: Cash equivalent cost given up is the basis for initial recording of elements.
Revenue: Record revenues when earned and measurable (exchange complete, earnings complete and collection probable).
Matching: Record expenses when incurred in earning revenue.
Full-disclosure: Disclose relevant economic information.

The Conceptual Framework

Constraints

Materiality: Relatively small amounts not likely to influence decisions are to be recorded in most cost/beneficial way.
Cost/Benefit: Benefits of recording and reporting information should outweigh costs.
Conservatism: Exercise care not to overstate assets and revenues or understate liabilities and expenses.
Industry peculiarities: Differences in accounting and reporting for certain items are permitted if there is a clear precedent in the industry.

Nature of Business Transactions

External events: exchanges of assets and liabilities between the business and one or more other parties.

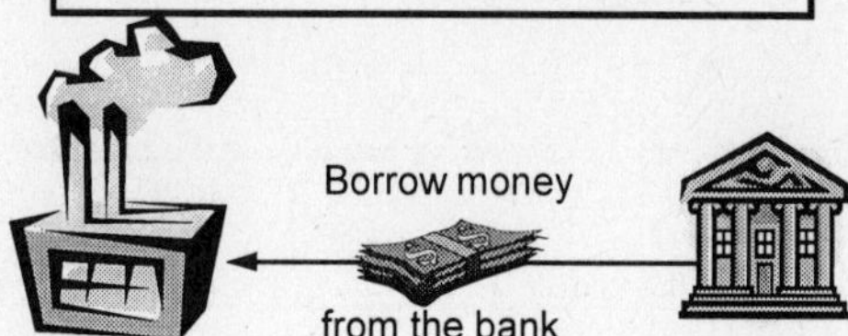

Nature of Business Transactions

Internal events: not an exchange between the business and other parties, but have a direct effect on the accounting entity.

Accounts

An organized format used by companies to accumulate the dollar effects of transactions.

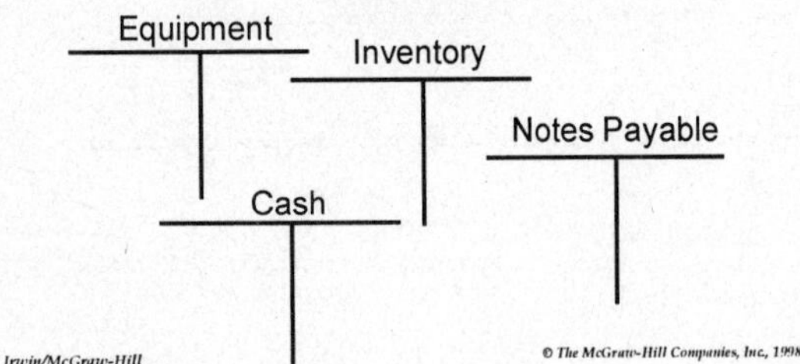

Transaction Analysis

❶Every transaction affects at least two accounts (duality of effects).

❷The accounting equation must remain in balance after each transaction.

A = L + SE

Duality of Effects

- Most transactions with external parties involve an exchange where the business entity both gives up something and receives something in return.

Maintain the Accounting Equation

❶ Identify the accounts affected and classify each as an asset, liability or equity account.
❷ Determine the effect (increase or decrease) on each account.
❸ Determine that the accounting equation remains in balance.

Maintain the Accounting Equation

Let's see how we keep the accounting equation in balance.

❶ Identify the Accounts Affected

Owners contribute $20,000 cash to start the business.

The two accounts involved are:

(1) Cash (asset)

(2) Contributed Capital (equity)

❷ Determine the Effect on Each Account

Owners contribute $20,000 cash to start the business.

- **The Cash account increases (+) by $20,000.**
- **The Contributed Capital account increases (+) by $20,000.**

❸ The Accounting Equation

Owners contribute $20,000 cash to start the business.

	Assets			=	Liabilities	+	Stockholders' Equity
	Cash	Equip.	Inv.		Accts. Pay.		Contributed Capital
Effect				=			

❸ The Accounting Equation

Owners contribute $20,000 cash to start the business.

	Assets			=	Liabilities	+	Stockholders' Equity
	Cash	Equip.	Inv.		Accts. Pay.		Contributed Capital
(A)	20,000						20,000
Effect		20,000		=			20,000

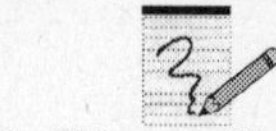

❶ Identify the Accounts Affected

Purchased equipment paying $4,500 cash.

The two accounts involved are:
(1) Cash (asset)
(2) Equipment (asset)

❷ Determine the Effect on Each Account

Purchased equipment paying $4,500 cash.

The Cash account decreases (-) by $4,500.
The Equipment account increases (+) by $4,500.

❸ The Accounting Equation

Purchased equipment paying $4,500 cash.

	Assets			=	Liabilities	+	Stockholders' Equity
	Cash	Equip.	Inv.		Accts. Pay.		Contributed Capital
(A)	20,000						20,000
Effect		20,000		=			20,000

❸ The Accounting Equation

Purchased equipment paying $4,500 cash.

	Assets			=	Liabilities	+	Stockholders' Equity
	Cash	Equip.	Inv.		Accts. Pay.		Contributed Capital
(A)	20,000						20,000
(B)	(4,500)	4,500					
Effect		20,000		=			20,000

Both of the accounts involved are on one side of the equation; the totals do not change.

❶ Identify the Accounts Affected

Purchase $1,000 of inventory on account.

The two accounts involved are:

(1) Inventory (asset)

(2) Accounts payable (liability)

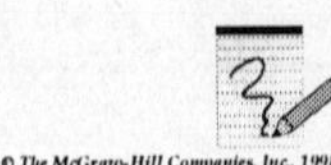

❷ Determine the Effect on Each Account

Purchase $1,000 of inventory on account.

The Inventory account increases (+) by $1,000.

The Accounts Payable account increases (+) by $1,000.

❸ The Accounting Equation

Purchase $1,000 of inventory on account.

	Assets			=	Liabilities	+	Stockholders' Equity
	Cash	Equip.	Inv.		Accts. Pay.		Contributed Capital
(A)	20,000						20,000
(B)	(4,500)	4,500					
Effect		20,000		=			20,000

❸ The Accounting Equation

Purchase $1,000 of inventory on account.

	Assets			=	Liabilities	+	Stockholders' Equity
	Cash	Equip.	Inv.		Accts. Pay.		Contributed Capital
(A)	20,000						20,000
(B)	(4,500)	4,500					
(C)			1,000		1,000		
Effect		21,000		=			21,000

When accounts are on opposite sides of the equation, the totals change.

❶ Identify the Accounts Affected

Paid $1,000 on account.

The two accounts involved are:
(1) Cash (asset)
(2) Accounts payable (liability)

❷ Determine the Effect on Each Account

Paid $1,000 on account.

The Cash account decreases (-) by $1,000.
The Accounts Payable account decreases (-) by $1,000.

❸ The Accounting Equation

Paid $1,000 on account.

	Assets			=	Liabilities	+	Stockholders' Equity
	Cash	Equip.	Inv.		Accts. Pay.		Contributed Capital
(A)	20,000						20,000
(B)	(4,500)	4,500					
(C)			1,000		1,000		
Effect		21,000		=			21,000

❸ The Accounting Equation

Paid $1,000 on account.

	Assets			= Liabilities	+ Stockholders' Equity
	Cash	Equip.	Inv.	Accts. Pay.	Contributed Capital
(A)	20,000				20,000
(B)	(4,500)	4,500			
(C)			1,000	1,000	
(D)	(1,000)			(1,000)	
Effect		20,000		=	20,000

Irwin/McGraw-Hill

How Do Companies Keep Track of Account Balances?

Irwin/McGraw-Hill

Direction of Transaction Effects

The left side of the T-account is always the debit side.

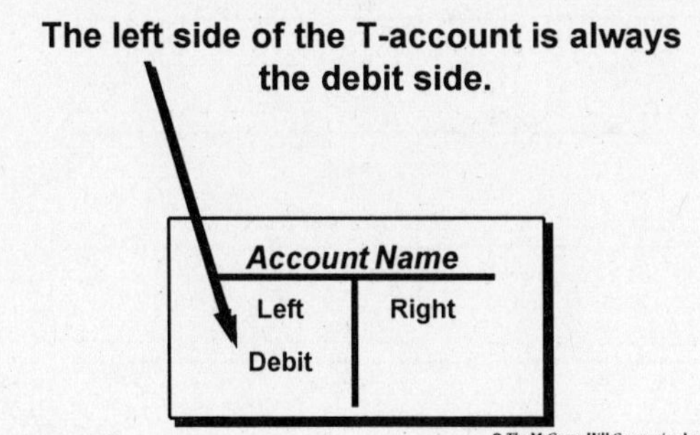

Irwin/McGraw-Hill

Direction of Transaction Effects

The right side of the T-account is always the credit side.

Account Name	
Left	Right
Debit	Credit

The Debit-Credit Framework

Debits and credits affect the Balance Sheet Model as follows:

A = L + SE

ASSETS		LIABILITIES		EQUITIES	
Debit for Increase	Credit for Decrease	Debit for Decrease	Credit for Increase	Debit for Decrease	Credit for Increase

Normal Balances

The normal balance for each type of account is:

Account Name	
Debit Balance	Credit Balance
Assets	Liabilities Stockholders' Equity

Analytical Tool: The Journal Entry

A typical journal looks like this:

GENERAL JOURNAL			Page 1		
Date		Description	Post. Ref.	Debit	Credit

Irwin/McGraw-Hill

Analytical Tool: The Journal Entry

A journal entry might look like this:

GENERAL JOURNAL			Page 1		
Date		Description	Post. Ref.	Debit	Credit
Jan.	1	Cash		20,000	
		Contributed Capital			20,000

Irwin/McGraw-Hill

Analytical Tool: The Journal Entry

Provide a reference date for each transaction.

Debits are written first.

GENERAL JOURNAL			Page 1		
Date		Description	Post. Ref.	Debit	Credit
Jan.	1	Cash		20,000	
		Contributed Capital			20,000

Credits are indented and written after debits.

Total debits must equal total credits.

Irwin/McGraw-Hill

Analytical Tool: The T-Account

After journal entries are prepared, the accountant posts (transfers) the dollar amounts to each account that was affected by the transaction.

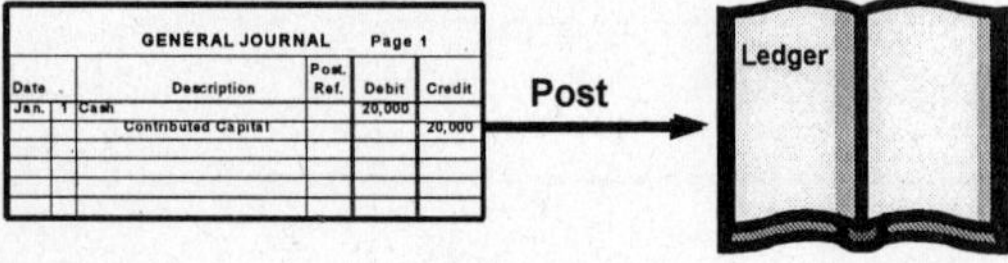

Transaction Analysis Illustrated

Let's examine some transactions that were completed on January 2, 1998.

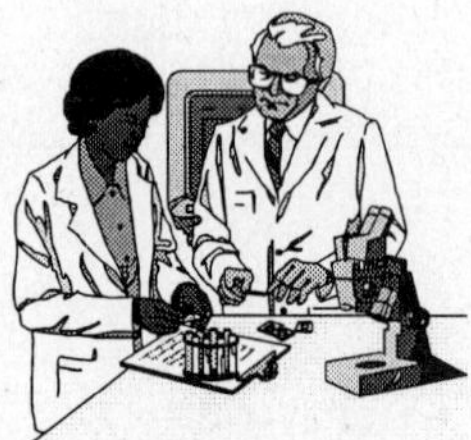

Example Transaction (A)

Owners invested $10,000 in a new business checking account in the name Webb, Inc.

Identify accounts, classifications, and effects, and determine how to record the increases and decreases using debits and credits.

Example Transaction (A)

Owners invested $10,000 in a new business checking account in the name Webb, Inc.

Account?	Cash	Account?	Contributed Capital
Class?	Asset	Class?	Stockholder's Equity
Effect?	+ $10,000	Effect?	+ $10,000
How?	Debit	How?	Credit

Example Transaction (A)

Owners invested $10,000 in a new business checking account in the name Webb, Inc.

GENERAL JOURNAL Page 1

Date		Description	Post. Ref.	Debit	Credit
Jan.	2	Cash		10,000	
		Contributed Capital			10,000

Example Transaction (A)

Owners invested $10,000 in a new business checking account in the name Webb, Inc.

Post the debits and credits in the T-Accounts.

Cash		Contributed Capital	
Dr.	Cr.	Dr.	Cr.

Example Transaction (A)

Owners invested $10,000 in a new business checking account in the name Webb, Inc.

Post the debits and credits in the T-Accounts.

Cash		Contributed Capital	
Dr.	Cr.	Dr.	Cr.
(A)+ 10,000			(A)+ 10,000

Example Transaction (B)

Webb, Inc. purchased equipment for which $6,000 in cash was paid.

Identify accounts, classifications, and effects, and determine how to record the increases and decreases using debits and credits.

Example Transaction (B)

Webb, Inc. purchased equipment for which $6,000 in cash was paid.

Account?	Cash	Account?	Equipment
Class?	Asset	Class?	Asset
Effect?	- $6,000	Effect?	+ $6,000
How?	Credit	How?	Debit

Example Transaction (B)

Webb, Inc. purchased equipment for which $6,000 in cash was paid.

GENERAL JOURNAL Page 1

Date		Description	Post. Ref.	Debit	Credit
Jan.	2	Equipment		6,000	
		Cash			6,000

Example Transaction (B)

Webb, Inc. purchased equipment for which $6,000 in cash was paid.

Post the debits and credits in the T-Accounts.

Cash Dr.	Cash Cr.	Equipment Dr.	Equipment Cr.
(A)+ 10,000	(B)- 6,000	(B)+ 6,000	

Example Transaction (C)

Webb, Inc. purchased $425 worth of sandpaper, chemicals, and other supplies, promising to pay in 30 days.

Identify accounts, classifications, and effects, and determine how to record the increases and decreases using debits and credits.

Example Transaction (C)

Webb, Inc. purchased $425 worth of sandpaper, chemicals, and other supplies, promising to pay in 30 days.

Account?	Accounts Payable	Account?	Supplies Inventory
Class?	Liability	Class?	Asset
Effect?	+ $425	Effect?	+ $425
How?	Credit	How?	Debit

Example Transaction (C)

Webb, Inc. purchased $425 worth of sandpaper, chemicals, and other supplies, promising to pay in 30 days.

GENERAL JOURNAL — Page 1

Date		Description	Post. Ref.	Debit	Credit
Jan.	2	Supplies Inventory		425	
		Accounts Payable			425

Example Transaction (C)

Webb, Inc. purchased $425 worth of sandpaper, chemicals, and other supplies, promising to pay in 30 days.

Post the debits and credits in the T-Accounts.

Supplies Inventory

Dr.	Cr.
(C)+ 425	

Accounts Payable

Dr.	Cr.
	(C)+ 425

Example Transaction (D)

Webb, Inc. borrows $1,200 from a local bank, signing a one-year promissory note.

Identify accounts, classifications, and effects, and determine how to record the increases and decreases using debits and credits.

Example Transaction (D)

Webb, Inc. borrows $1,200 from a local bank, signing a one-year promissory note.

Account?	Cash	Account?	Notes Payable
Class?	Asset	Class?	Liability
Effect?	+ $1,200	Effect?	+ $1,200
How?	Debit	How?	Credit

Example Transaction (D)

Webb, Inc. borrows $1,200 from a local bank, signing a one-year promissory note.

GENERAL JOURNAL Page 1

Date		Description	Post. Ref.	Debit	Credit
Jan.	2	Cash		1,200	
		Notes Payable			1,200

Example Transaction (D)

Webb, Inc. borrows $1,200 from a local bank, signing a one-year promissory note.

Post the debits and credits in the T-Accounts.

Cash		Notes Payable	
Dr.	Cr.	Dr.	Cr.
(A)+ 10,000	(B)- 6,000		(D)+ 1,200
(D)+ 1,200			

Irwin/McGraw-Hill

Example Transaction (E)

Webb, Inc. paid $425 to a creditor on account.

Identify accounts, classifications, and effects, and determine how to record the increases and decreases using debits and credits.

Irwin/McGraw-Hill

Example Transaction (E)

Webb, Inc. paid $425 to a creditor on account.

Account?	Cash	Account?	Accts. payable
Class?	Asset	Class?	Liability
Effect?	- $425	Effect?	- $425
How?	Credit	How?	Debit

Irwin/McGraw-Hill

Example Transaction (E)

Webb, Inc. paid $425 to a creditor on account.

GENERAL JOURNAL Page 1

Date		Description	Post. Ref.	Debit	Credit
Jan.	2	Accounts Payable		425	
		Cash			425

Example Transaction (E)

Webb, Inc. paid $425 to a creditor on account.

Post the debits and credits in the T-Accounts.

Cash		Accounts Payable	
Dr.	Cr.	Dr.	Cr.
(A)+10,000	(B) - 6,000	(E)- 425	(C)+ 425
(D) + 1,200	(E) - 425		

Question

The Cash account has four entries: debits of $10,000 and $1,200, and credits of $6,000 and $425. What is the balance in the Cash account?

a. $ 17,625 Debit
b. $ 4,775 Credit
c. $ 4,775 Debit
d. $ 11,200 Debit

Balance Sheet Preparation

It is possible to prepare a balance sheet at any point in time.

Some Misconceptions

Don't confuse bookkeeping with accounting. Bookkeeping involves the routine, clerical part of accounting and requires only minimal knowledge of accounting, but . . .

An **accountant** is a trained professional who can design information systems, analyze complex transactions, and interpret financial data.

Some Misconceptions

Are all transactions subject to precise and objective measurement?

Almost all accounting numbers are influenced by estimates.

Some Misconceptions

Some people believe that financial statements report the market value of the company.

But financial statements really report the **cost** of assets, liabilities and stockholders' equity

End of Chapter

3

OPERATING DECISIONS AND THE INCOME STATEMENT

Business Background

Businesses develop . . .

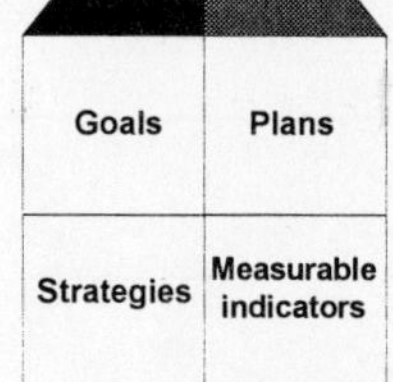

The goals include elements of income.

Business Background

What business activities affect the income statement?

How are each of these activities measured?

How are these activities reported on the income statement?

The Conceptual Framework

Assumptions

Separate-entity: Transactions of the business are separate from transactions of owners.
Unit-of-measure: Accounting measures are in the national monetary unit ($).
Continuity: The entity will not go out of business in the near future.
Time-period: The long life of a company can be reported over a series of shorter time periods.

The Conceptual Framework

To meet the needs of decision makers, we report financial information for relatively short time periods (monthly, quarterly, annually).

Life of the Business

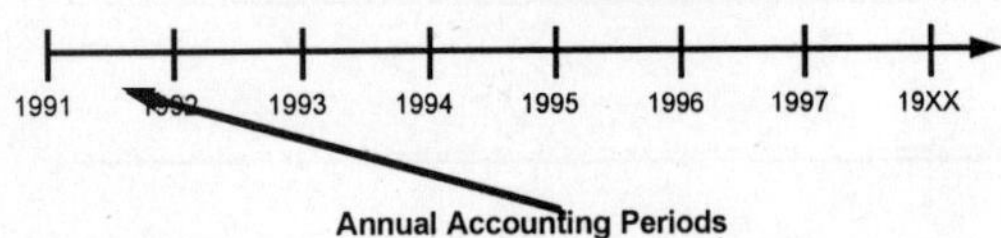

The Conceptual Framework

Elements of Financial Statements

Assets: Probable future economic benefits owned by the entity from past transactions.
Liabilities: Debts or obligations from past transactions to be paid with assets or services.
Stockholders' Equity: Financing provided by owners and operations.
Revenues: Inflows of net assets from ongoing operations.
Expenses: Outflows of net assets from ongoing operations.
Gains: Inflows of net assets from peripheral transactions.
Losses: Outflows of net assets from peripheral transactions.

SAMPLE COMPANY Statement of Income For the Year Ended December 31, 1999 (In thousands of dollars, except for per share data)		
Revenues:		
Sales		$ 52,500
Interest		485
Total revenues		$ 52,985
Costs and expenses:		
Cost of merchandise sold	$ 24,600	
Payroll expense	12,500	
Rent expense	2,000	
Depreciation expense	950	
General and administrative expense	3,500	
Total costs and expenses		43,550
Income before income taxes		9,435
Income taxes		3,100
Net income		6,335
Earning per share		$ 2.08

Irwin/ McGraw-Hill

SAMPLE COMPANY Statement of Income For the Year Ended December 31, 1999 (In thousands of dollars, except for per share data)		
Revenues:		
Sales		$ 52,500
Interest		485
Total revenues		$ 52,985
Costs and expenses:		
Cost of merchandise sold	$ 24,600	
Payroll expense	12,500	
Rent expense	2,000	
Total costs and expenses		43,550
Income before income taxes		9,435
Income taxes		3,100
Net income		6,335
Earning per share		$ 2.08

Net income = Total revenues - Total expenses

Irwin/ McGraw-Hill

Principles Affecting Income Determination

1. **The revenue principle.**
2. **The matching principle.**
3. **The cost principle.**

Irwin/ McGraw-Hill

The Conceptual Framework

Principles

Cost: Cash equivalent cost given up is the basis for initial recording of elements.
Revenue: Record revenues when earned and measurable (exchange complete, earnings complete and collection probable).
Matching: Record expenses when incurred in earning revenue.
Full-disclosure: Disclose relevant economic information.

Income Measurement

The Operating Cycle

1	2	3	4
Purchase merchandise from supplier.	Pay supplier for merchandise.	Sell merchandise to customer.	Collect cash from customer.

Time

Income Measurement

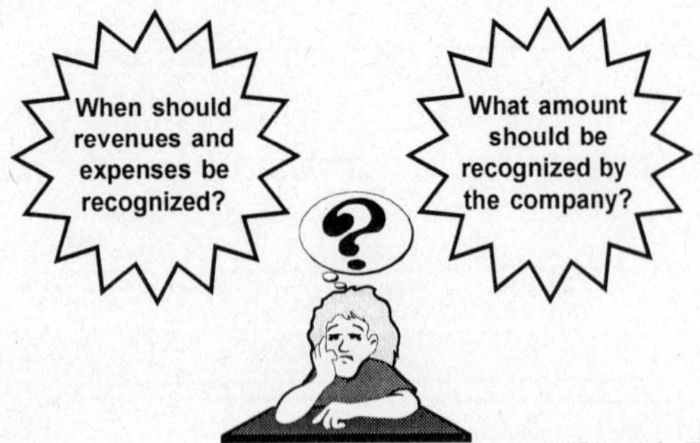

When should revenues and expenses be recognized?
What amount should be recognized by the company?
?

Cash Basis Accounting

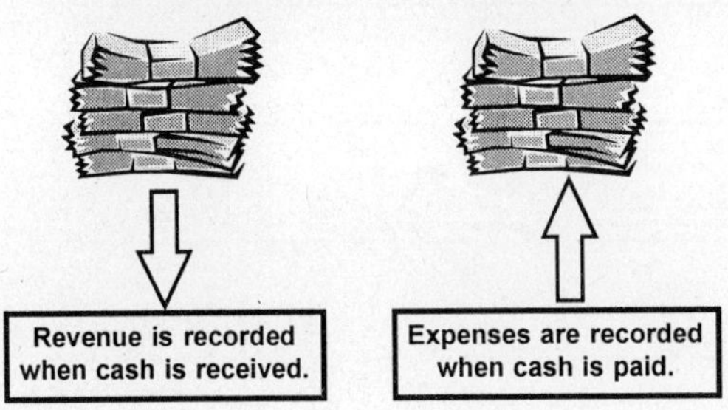

Accrual Basis Accounting

Revenue principle

Recognize revenues when . . .

❶Earnings process is complete or nearly complete,
❷An exchange transaction takes place, and
❸Collection is reasonably assured.

The Revenue Principle

Typical liabilities that become revenue when earned include . . .

Liability (cash received before being earned)	Becomes	Revenue (earned when good or service provided)
Rent collected in advance	→	Rent revenue
Unearned air traffic revenue	→	Air traffic revenue
Deferred subscription revenue	→	Subscription revenue

The Revenue Principle

Assets reflecting revenues earned but not yet received in cash include . . .

Asset (resource)	Resulting From	Revenue (earned before cash is received)
Interest receivable	→	Interest revenue
Rent receivable	→	Rent revenue
Royalties receivable	→	Royalty revenue

Accrual Basis Accounting

Matching principle

Resources consumed to earn revenues in an accounting period should be recorded in that period, regardless of when cash is paid.

Matching Principle

Assets and their related expense accounts include. . .

Asset (resource)	Becomes	Expense (when resource is used)
Supplies inventory	→	Supplies expense
Prepaid insurance	→	Insurance expense
Buildings and equipment	→	Depreciation expense

Matching Principle

Liabilities and their related expense accounts include . . .

Liability	Resulting from	Expense (incurred before cash paid)
Salaries payable	→	Salaries expense
Interest payable	→	Interest expense
Property taxes payable	→	Property tax expense

Question

On June 30, 1998, Telecom, Inc. purchased a one-year fire insurance policy by paying $1,200 cash. If Telecom is a cash basis company, how much insurance expense will be recognized in 1998?

a. $1,200
b. $600
c. $0

Question

On June 30, 1998, Telecom, Inc. purchased a one-year fire insurance policy by paying $1,200 cash. If Telecom is an accrual basis company, how much insurance expense will be recognized in 1998?

a. $1,200
b. $600
c. $0

The Accounting Cycle

To compensate for differences between the operating cycle, cash flow dates, and accounting cycle, it is necessary to prepare adjusting entries.

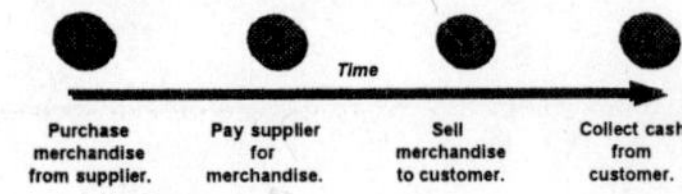

Irwin/ McGraw-Hill

The Accounting Cycle

Start of the Accounting Period

During the Accounting Period.	**1. Perform transaction analysis. 2. Record journal entries. 3. Post amounts to general ledger.**
End of the Accounting Period.	**1. Prepare a trial balance. 2. Record and post adjusting entries. 3. Prepare financial statements. 4. Record and post closing entries.**

End of the Accounting Period

Irwin/ McGraw-Hill

Completion of the Transaction Analysis Model

A = L + SE

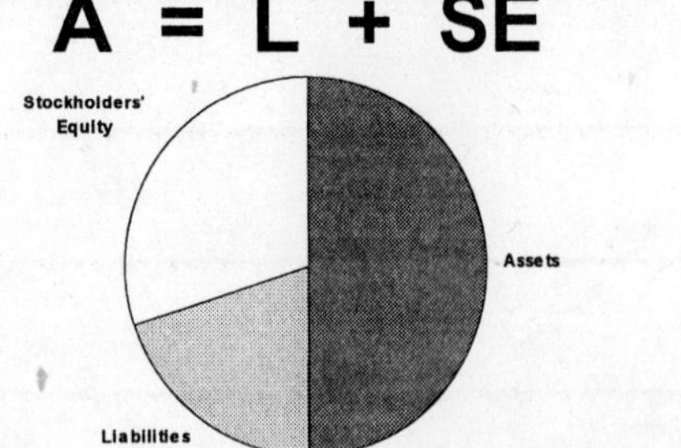

Irwin/ McGraw-Hill

Completion of the Transaction Analysis Model

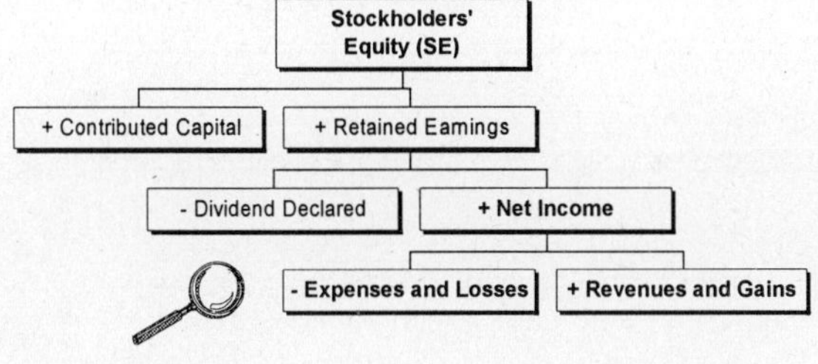

Completion of the Transaction Analysis Model

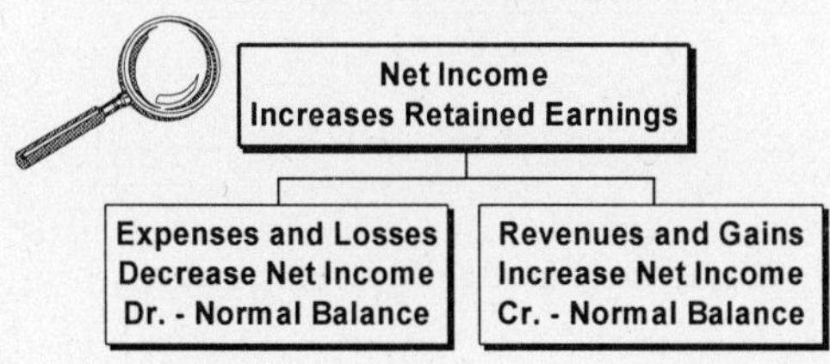

Transaction Analysis

On May 8, Jenkins Company provided services to Maxtel, Inc. and was paid $1,275 cash.

Transaction Analysis							
Assets		=	Liabilities	+	Stockholders' Equity	
Cash	+$1,275				Revenue	+$1,275

Transaction Analysis

On May 8, Jenkins Company provided services to Maxtel, Inc. and was paid $1,275 cash.

Transaction Analysis

Assets		=	Liabilities	+	Stockholders' Equity	
Cash	+$1,275				Revenue	+$1,275

Date		Description	Post. Ref.	Debit	Credit
May	8	Cash		1,275	
		Service Revenue			1,275

Transaction Analysis

On May 8, Jenkins Company provided services to Maxtel, Inc. and was paid $1,275 cash.

Post the debits and credits in the T-accounts.

Cash		Service Revenue	
Dr.	Cr.	Dr.	Cr.
1,275			1,275

Transaction Analysis

On May 9, Jenkins Co. paid $500 cash for May's rent.

Transaction Analysis

Assets		=	Liabilities	+	Stockholders' Equity	
Cash	-$500				Rent expense	-$500

Transaction Analysis

On May 9, Jenkins Co. paid $500 cash for May's rent.

Transaction Analysis				
Assets	=	Liabilities	+	Stockholders' Equity
Cash -$500				Rent expense -$500

GENERAL JOURNAL				Page 12	
Date		Description	Post. Ref.	Debit	Credit
May	9	Rent Expense		500	
		Cash			500

Irwin/ McGraw-Hill

Transaction Analysis

On May 9, Jenkins Co. paid $500 cash for May's rent.

Post the debits and credits in the T-accounts.

Cash		Rent Expense	
Dr.	Cr.	Dr.	Cr.
1,275	500	500	

Irwin/ McGraw-Hill

Transaction Analysis

On May 16, Jenkins Co. provided services to Maxtel, Inc. and Maxtel promised to pay the $1,000 in 30 days.

Transaction Analysis				
Assets	=	Liabilities	+	Stockholders' Equity
Receivables +$1,000				Revenues +$1,000

Irwin/ McGraw-Hill

Transaction Analysis

On May 16, Jenkins Co. provided services to Maxtel, Inc. and Maxtel promised to pay the $1,000 in 30 days.

Transaction Analysis				
Assets	=	Liabilities	+	Stockholders' Equity
Receivables +$1,000				Revenues +$1,000

GENERAL JOURNAL				Page 12	
Date		Description	Post. Ref.	Debit	Credit
May	16	Accounts Receivable		1,000	
		Service Revenue			1,000

Transaction Analysis

On May 16, Jenkins Co. provided services to Maxtel, Inc. and Maxtel promised to pay the $1,000 in 30 days.

Post the debits and credits in the T-accounts.

Accounts Receivable		Service Revenue	
Dr.	Cr.	Dr.	Cr.
1,000			1,275
			1,000

Transaction Analysis

On May 20, Jenkins Co. purchased $135 of office supplies and promised to pay for them in 30 days.

Transaction Analysis				
Assets	=	Liabilities	+	Stockholders' Equity
Supplies $135		Payables $135		

Transaction Analysis

On May 20, Jenkins Co. purchased $135 of office supplies and promised to pay for them in 30 days.

Transaction Analysis

Assets		=	Liabilities		+	Stockholders' Equity
Supplies	$135		Payables	$135		

GENERAL JOURNAL — Page 12

Date		Description	Post. Ref.	Debit	Credit
May	20	Office Supplies		135	
		Accounts Payable			135

Irwin/ McGraw-Hill

Transaction Analysis

On May 20, Jenkins Co. purchased $135 of office supplies and promised to pay for them in 30 days.

Post the debits and credits in the T-accounts.

Office Supplies		Accounts Payable	
Dr.	Cr.	Dr.	Cr.
135			135

Irwin/ McGraw-Hill

Transaction Analysis

On May 30, Jenkins Co. paid its telephone bill of $30 and received its water bill for June in the amount of $18.

Transaction Analysis

Assets		=	Liabilities		+	Stockholders' Equity
Cash	-$30		Payables	+$18		Utilities expense -$48

Irwin/ McGraw-Hill

Transaction Analysis

On May 30, Jenkins Co. paid its telephone bill of $30 and received its water bill for June in the amount of $18.

Transaction Analysis				
Assets	=	Liabilities	+	Stockholders' Equity
Cash -$30		Payables +$18		Utilities expense -$48

GENERAL JOURNAL				Page 12	
Date		Description	Post. Ref.	Debit	Credit
May	30	Utilities Expense		48	
		Accounts Payable			18
		Cash			30

Transaction Analysis

On May 30, Jenkins Co. paid its telephone bill of $30 and received its water bill for June in the amount of $18.

Post the debits and credits in the T-accounts.

Utilities Expense

Dr.	Cr.
48	

Cash

Dr.	Cr.
1,275	500 30

Accounts Payable

Dr.	Cr.
	135 18

Income Statement Preparation

After all journal entries have been made and posted to the T-accounts, we can prepare the income statement for the period.

Jenkins Co.
Income Statement
For the Month Ended May 31, 1999

Service revenue	$ 2,275
Operating expenses:	
Rent expense	500
Utilities expense	48
Net income	$ 1,727

Statement of Stockholders' Equity

Net income is the amount that ties the income statement to the balance sheet.

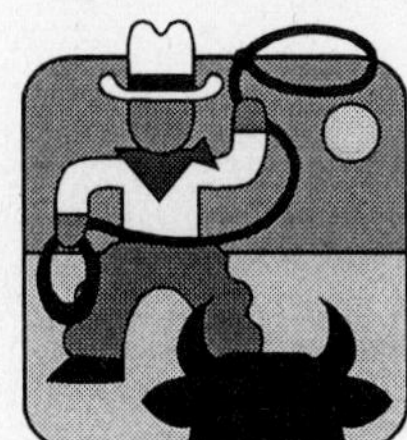

Sample Company
Statement of Stockholders' Equity
for the Period Ended June 30, 1998
(in thousands of dollars)

	Contributed Capital	Retained Earnings	Total
Balance, January 1, 1998	$ 30,500	$155,100	$185,600
Additional stock issued	200		200
Net income		17,960	17,960
Dividends declared		(2,000)	(2,000)
Balance, June 30, 1998	$ 30,700	$171,060	$201,760

Net income is part of Retained Earnings, and Retained Earnings is in the equity section of the balance sheet.

End of Chapter 3

4

THE ADJUSTMENT PROCESS AND FINANCIAL STATEMENTS

Business Background

Companies usually record external transactions when the business documents supporting the transactions are processed.

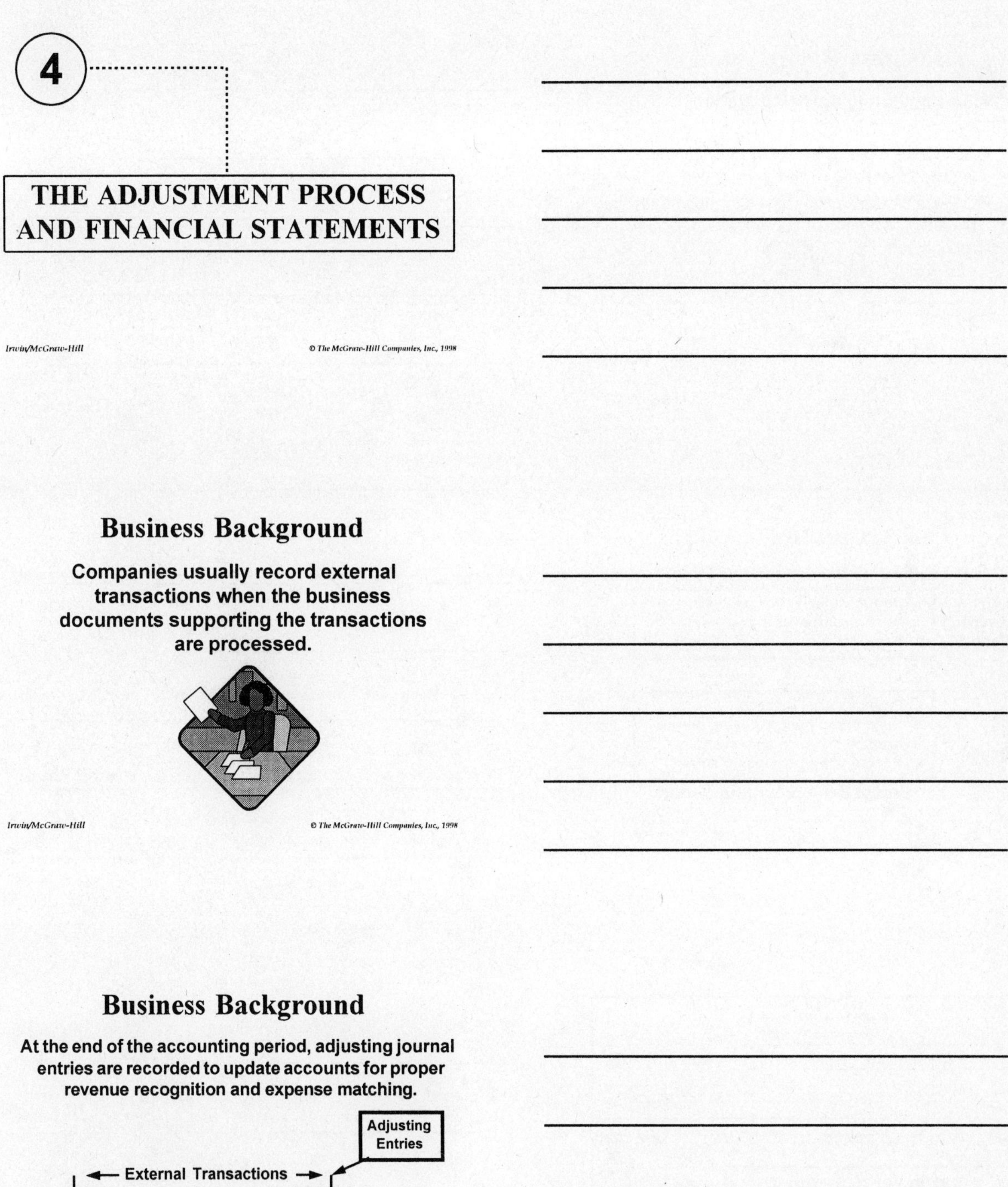

Business Background

At the end of the accounting period, adjusting journal entries are recorded to update accounts for proper revenue recognition and expense matching.

Adjusting Entries

External Transactions

Start of Accounting Period

End of Accounting Period

Business Background

The adjusting entries include . . .

❶Accruals - Revenues earned or expenses incurred that have not been recorded.

❷Deferrals - Receipts of assets or payments of cash in advance of revenue or expense recognition.

The Accounting Cycle

Start of the Accounting Period

During the Accounting Period.

1. Perform transaction analysis.
2. Record journal entries.
3. Post amounts to general ledger.

End of the Accounting Period.

1. Prepare a trial balance.
2. Record and post adjusting entries.
3. Prepare financial statements.
4. Record and post closing entries.

End of the Accounting Period

SPENCER, INC.
Unadjusted Trial Balance
December 31, 1998

Description	Debit	Credit
Cash	$ 3,900	
Accounts receivable	4,985	
Inventory	3,300	
Office equipment	4,800	
Accumulated depreciation - Office equip.		$ 1,440
Furniture and fixtures	6,600	
Accu		2,200
Acco		2,985
Note		4,000
Com		10,000
Retained earnings		2,960
Totals	$ 23,585	$ 23,585

A listing of all accounts showing their ending balances.

SPENCER, INC.
Unadjusted Trial Balance
December 31, 1998

Description	Debit	Credit
Cash	$ 3,900	
Accounts receivable	4,985	
I	3,300	
O	4,800	
A		$ 1,440
F	6,600	
Accumulated depreciation - Furn. & fix.		2,200
Accounts payable		2,985
Notes payable		4,000
Common stock		10,000
Retained earnings		2,960
Totals	$ 23,585	$ 23,585

The primary purpose of the trial balance is to show that total debits equal total credits.

SPENCER, INC.
Unadjusted Trial Balance
8

Description	Debit	Credit
	$ 3,900	
	4,985	
	3,300	
Office equipment	4,800	
Accumulated depreciation - Office equip.		$ 1,440
Furniture and fixtures	6,600	
Accumulated depreciation - Furn. & fix.		2,200
Accounts payable		2,985
Notes payable		4,000
Common stock		10,000
Retained earnings		2,960
Totals	$ 23,585	$ 23,585

Accumulated depreciation is a contra-asset account. It is directly related to an asset account but has the opposite balance.

Trial Balance

Contra-asset

Office equipment	$ 4,800
Accumulated depreciation - Office equip.	(1,440)
Book value	$ 3,360

The cost of a long-lived asset less its accumulated depreciation is called ***Book Value***.

Trial Balance

If total debits do not equal total credits on the trial balance, errors have occurred . . .

- in preparing balanced journal entries.
- in posting the correct dollar effects of a transaction.
- in copying ending balances from the ledger to the trial balance.

Irwin/McGraw-Hill

Now that we have covered the trial balance, let's discuss adjusting entries.
Adjusting Entries

Irwin/McGraw-Hill

Deferrals

End of accounting period.

Cash received or paid. → Revenues earned or expense incurred

- Rent collected in advance of occupancy.
- Insurance premium paid in advance.

Irwin/McGraw-Hill

Accruals

End of accounting period.

Revenues earned or expense incurred

Cash received or paid.

Services performed in advance of collection.

Wages earned by employees but not yet paid.

Deferrals

On January 1, 1998, Tipton, Inc. purchased a 3-year fire insurance policy paying $3,600 cash.

Tipton recorded the purchase with the following entry . . .

Deferrals

On January 1, 1998, Tipton, Inc. purchased a 3-year fire insurance policy paying $3,600 cash.

GENERAL JOURNAL Page 24

Date		Description	PR	Debit	Credit
Jan.	1	Prepaid Insurance Expense		3,600	
		Cash			3,600

This is an asset account.

Deferrals

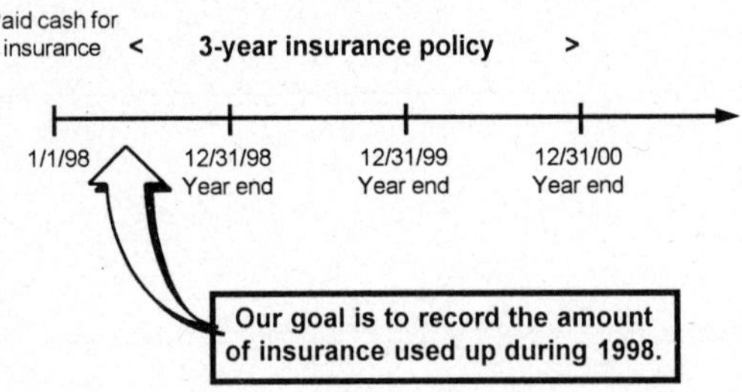

Irwin/McGraw-Hill

Deferrals

On January 1, 1998, Tipton, Inc. purchased a 3-year fire insurance policy paying $3,600 cash.

GENERAL JOURNAL Page 24

Date		Description	PR	Debit	Credit
Jan.	1	Prepaid Insurance Expense		3,600	
		Cash			3,600

During 1998, Tipton used up 1/3 of the insurance coverage, so we need to record 1/3 of the total cost as an expense in 1998.

Irwin/McGraw-Hill

Deferrals

Adjusting entry at December 31, 1998, to recognize 1/3 of total insurance costs.

GENERAL JOURNAL Page 77

Date		Description	PR	Debit	Credit
Dec.	31	Insurance Expense		1,200	
		Prepaid Insurance Expense			1,200

$3,600 ÷ 3 years = $1,200 per year

Irwin/McGraw-Hill

Deferrals

After we post the entry to the T-accounts, the account balances look like this:

Prepaid Insurance Expense		Insurance Expense	
1/1 3,600	12/31 1,200	12/31 1,200	
Bal. 2,400		Bal. 1,200	

Deferrals

Now, let's look at an example of cash received in advance.

Deferrals

On December 1, 1998, Tom's Rentals received a check for $3,000, for the first three months' rent of a new tenant.

GENERAL JOURNAL Page 16

Date		Description	PR	Debit	Credit
Dec.	1	Cash		3,000	
		Unearned Rental Income			3,000

This account is a liability.

Deferrals

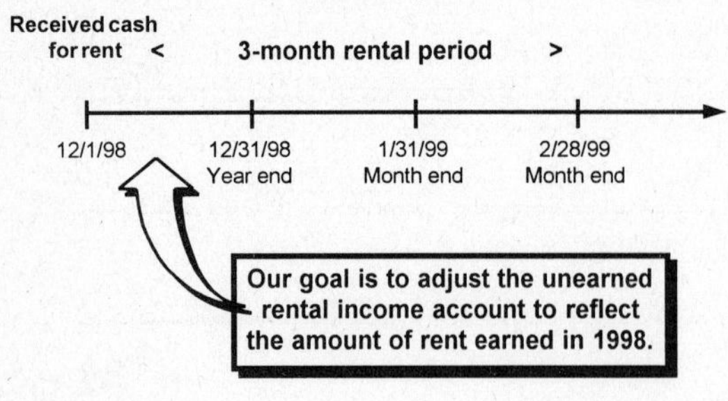

Deferrals

Adjusting entry on December 31 to adjust unearned rental account.

GENERAL JOURNAL Page 97

Date		Description	PR	Debit	Credit
Dec.	31	Unearned Rental Income		1,000	
		Rental Income			1,000

$3,000 ÷ 3 months = $1,000 per month.

Deferrals

After we post the entry to the T-accounts, the account balances look like this:

Unearned Rental Income (Debit)	Unearned Rental Income (Credit)
12/31 1,000	12/1 3,000
	Bal. 2,000

Rental Income (Debit)	Rental Income (Credit)
	12/31 1,000
	Bal. 1,000

Accruals

Now, we need to look at adjusting entries for accruals.

Accruals

Accruals occur when revenues have been earned or expenses incurred but no cash has been exchanged.

Irwin/McGraw-Hill
© The McGraw-Hill Companies, Inc., 1998

Accruals

On November 1, 1998, Webb, Inc. invests $10,000 for 3 months in a money market account that pays 12% interest per year. Webb, Inc. is a December 31 year-end company.

Let's record the adjusting entry on December 31, 1998 to record the interest earned but not yet received.

Irwin/McGraw-Hill
© The McGraw-Hill Companies, Inc., 1998

Accruals

On November 1, 1998, Webb, Inc. invests $10,000 for 3 months in a money market account that pays 12% interest per year. Webb, Inc. is a December 31 year-end company.

GENERAL JOURNAL Page 12

Date		Description	PR	Debit	Credit
Dec.	31	Interest Receivable		200	
		Interest Revenue			200

$10,000 × .12 = $1,200 per year ÷ 12 = $100 per month
$100 × 2 months = $200

Accruals

Denton, Inc. pays its employees every Friday. Year-end, 12/31/98, falls on a Wednesday. The employees have earned salaries of $47,250 for Monday through Wednesday of the week ended 12/31/98.

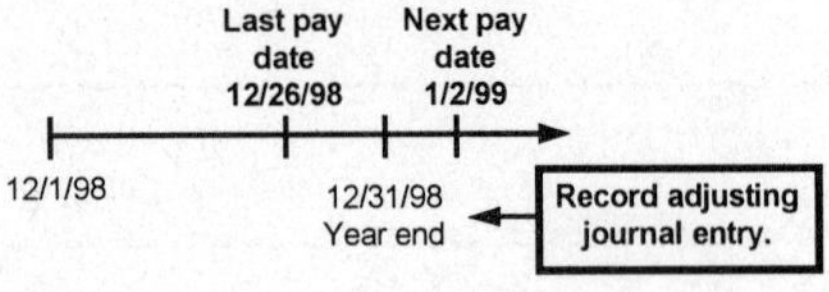

Accruals

Denton, Inc. pays its employees every Friday. Year-end, 12/31/98, falls on a Wednesday. The employees have earned salaries of $47,250 for Monday through Wednesday of the week ended 12/31/98.

GENERAL JOURNAL Page 87

Date		Description	PR	Debit	Credit
Dec.	31	Salaries Expense		47,250	
		Salaries Payable			47,250

Accounting Estimates

Certain circumstances require adjusting entries to record accounting estimates.

Examples include . . .

- **-- Depreciation**
- **-- Bad debts**
- **-- Income taxes**

$$$

Estimates

On January 1, 1998, Webb Co. purchased a truck for $23,000 cash. The truck has a useful life of 5 years and $1,000 residual value.

First, let's calculate the amount of depreciation using the straight-line method and make the necessary adjusting entry.

Estimates

On January 1, 1998, Webb Co. purchased a truck for $23,000 cash. The truck has a useful life of 5 years and $1,000 residual value.

$$\frac{\text{asset cost - residual value}}{\text{estimated useful life}} = \text{Depreciation expense for the period.}$$

$$\frac{(\$23{,}000 - \$1{,}000)}{5} = \$4{,}400$$

Estimates

On January 1, 1998, Webb Co. purchased a truck for $23,000 cash. The truck has a useful life of 5 years and $1,000 residual value.

GENERAL JOURNAL				Page 43	
Date		Description	PR	Debit	Credit
Dec.	31	Depreciation Expense		4,400	
		Accumulated Depreciation			4,400

This is a contra account.

Financial Statement Preparation

The next step in the accounting cycle is to prepare the financial statements. . .

- ❖Income statement,
- ❖Statement of stockholders' equity,
- ❖Balance sheet, and
- ❖Statement of cash flows.

Income Statement

Revenues
+ Gains
- Expenses
- Losses
= Net Income

- •Revenues
- • service revenue
- • interest revenue
- • sales revenue
- •Expenses
- • salary expense
- • utility expense
- • rent expense
- • tax expense

Allied Resellers, Inc. Income Statement For the Month Ended January 31, 1999 (in thousands of dollars)		
Sales revenue		$25,800
Rent revenue		630
Misc. revenue		50
Total revenues		26,480
Cost of goods sold	$2,720	
Payroll and other employee benefits	6,600	
Rent and other expenses	6,505	
Depreciation expense	2,400	
General and administrative expenses	90	
Total cost and expenses		18,315
Income before interest and income taxes		8,165
Interest expense		10
Income before income taxes		8,155
Income taxes		3,180
Net income		$ 4,975
Earnings per share		$ 0.40

Income Statement

Earnings per share (EPS) is reported on the income statement.

$$\text{EPS} = \frac{\text{Net Income}}{\text{Weighted-average number of common shares outstanding during the period}}$$

Statement of Stockholders' Equity

Net income appears on the statement of stockholders' equity as an increase in Retained Earnings.

Allied Resellers, Inc. Statement of Stockholders' Equity For the Month Ended January 31, 1999 (in thousands of dollars)	Contributed Capital	Retained Earnings	Total
Balance, December 31, 1998	$ 30,500	$ 155,100	$ 185,600
Additional stock issuance	200		200
Net income		4,975	4,975
Dividends declared		(2,000)	(2,000)
Balance, January 31, 1999	$ 30,700	$ 158,075	$ 188,775

Balance Sheet

A = L + SE

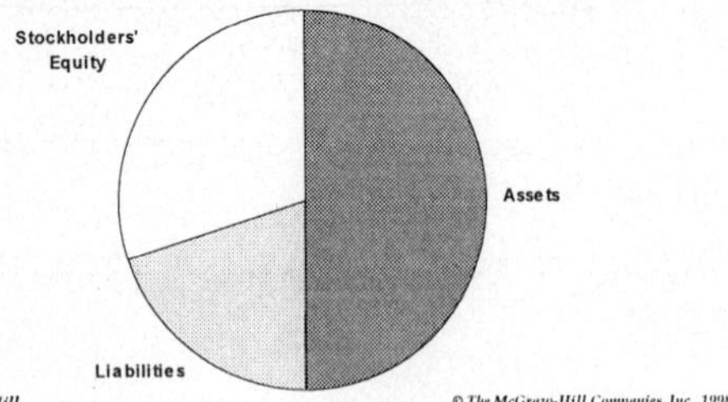

Balance Sheet

Allied Resellers, Inc.
Balance Sheet
at December 31, 1999 and 1998
(in thousands of dollars)

Assets	1999	1998
Cash	$ 89,680	$ 93,500
Marketable securities	10,000	10,000
Receivables (franchise fees and other)	3,280	2,600
Inventories	2,670	2,800
Prepaid expenses	14,700	1,700
Property and equipment	125,250	126,800
Other assets	5,300	5,300
Total assets	$ 250,880	$ 242,700

Continued

Allied Resellers, Inc.
Balance Sheet
at December 31, 1999 and 1998
(in thousands of dollars)

Liabilities	1999	1998
Accounts and notes payable	$ 11,130	$ 7,400
Accrued expenses payable (rent, payroll and other)	27,755	27,000
Dividend and interest payable	5,910	3,900
Income taxes payable	3,180	4,700
Unearned revenue	30	-
Deferred income taxes	14,100	14,100
Total Liabilities	$ 62,105	$ 57,100
Stockholders' Equity		
Contributed capital	30,700	30,500
Retained earnings	158,075	155,100
Total stockholders' equity	188,775	185,600
Total liabilities and stockholders' equity	$ 250,880	$ 242,700

Statement of Cash Flows

This statement describes the changes in cash for the period by showing changes in . . .

❶ Operating activities,
❷ Investing activities, and
❸ Financing activities.

Statement of Cash Flows

Operating activities include the. . .

Sale of services or goods to customers and related costs.

Payment of interest on debt and income taxes.

Statement of Cash Flows

Investing activities include . . .

Purchase and sale of long-term investments.

Loans to others.

Purchase and sale of long-term assets.

Statement of Cash Flows

Financing activities include the. . .

Issuing of debt or stock.

Repayment of debt.

Repurchase of stock.

Payment of dividends.

Allied Resellers, Inc. Statement of Cash Flows For the Month Ended January 31, 1999 (in thousands of dollars)	
Operating activities:	
Cash inflows from customers	$ 25,830
Cash outflows:	
to suppliers	(19,660)
to employees	(6,000)
for income taxes	(4,700)
Net cash used by operating activities	(4,530)
Investing activities:	
Cash inflows to repay loan to employee	40
Cash outflows:	
Purchase of equipment	(190)
Loan to employee	(40)
Net cash used in investing activities	(190)

Allied Resellers, Inc. Statement of Cash Flows - continued For the Month Ended January 31, 1999 (in thousands of dollars)	
Net cash used in investing activities	$ (190)
Financing activities:	
Cash inflows:	
Proceeds from bank borrowing	1,000
Additional stock issuance	200
Cash outflows to repay bank note	(300)
Net cash provided by financing activities	900
Increase in cash	(3,820)
Cash at the beginning of the month	93,500
Cash at the end of the month	$ 89,680

The Closing Process

The following accounts are called temporary or nominal accounts and are closed at the end of the period . . .

- Revenues
- Expenses
- Gains,
- Losses, and
- Dividends declared.

The Closing Process

Assets, liabilities, and stockholders' equity are permanent or real accounts and are never closed.

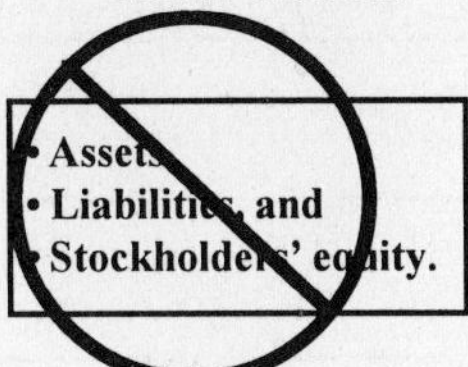

The Closing Process

Two steps are used in the closing process . . .

❶ Close revenues and gains to Retained Earnings.

❷ Close expenses and losses to Retained Earnings.

The Closing Process

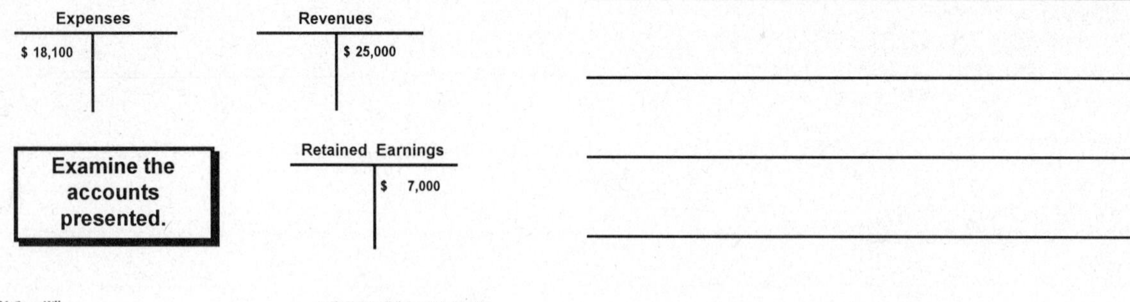

The Closing Process

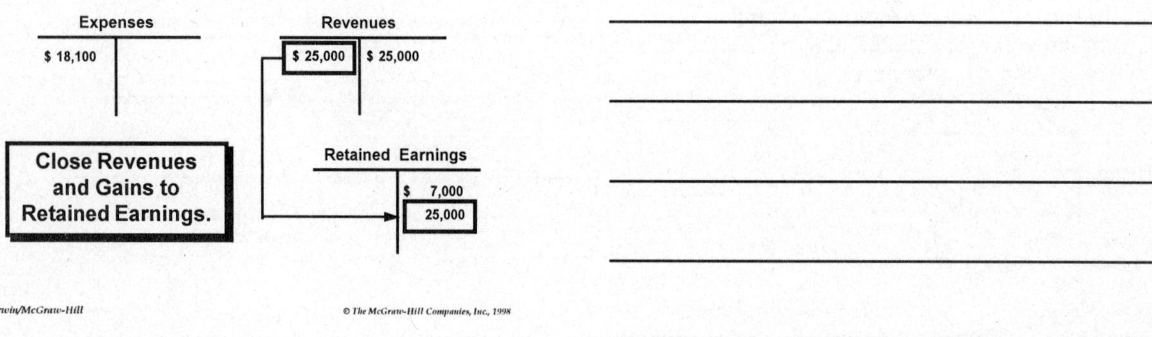

The Closing Process

Expenses

$ 18,100

Revenues

$ 25,000	$ 25,000
	$ -0-

Retained Earnings

	$ 7,000
	25,000

Close Expenses and Losses to Retained Earnings.

The Closing Process

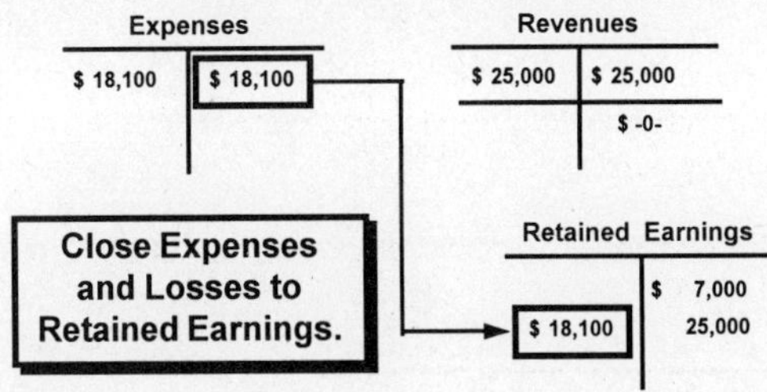

The Closing Process

Expenses

$ 18,100	$ 18,100
$ -0-	

Revenues

$ 25,000	$ 25,000
	$ -0-

Determine the balance in Retained Earnings.

Retained Earnings

	$ 7,000
$ 18,100	25,000
	$ 13,900

The Accounting Process and Communication Process

Preparing the financial statements is just the beginning of the communication process.

End of Chapter 4

THE COMMUNICATION OF ACCOUNTING INFORMATION

Who are the players in the accounting communication process?

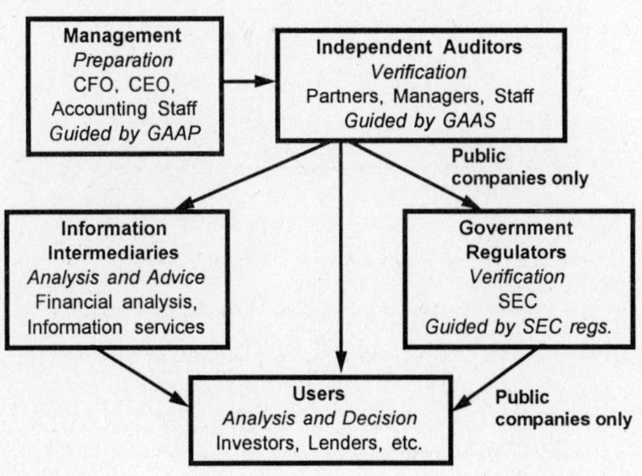

Conceptual Framework

Primary Objective of External Financial Reporting
To provide economic information to external users for decision making.

Primary Qualitative Characteristics
Relevance: Timely and Predictive and Feedback Value
Reliability: Accurate, Unbiased, and Verifiable

Secondary Qualitative Characteristics
Comparability: Across businesses
Consistency: Over time

Conceptual Framework

Constraints of Accounting

Materiality

Cost-Benefit

Conservatism

Industry Practices

Conceptual Framework Question

According to the conceptual framework, relevant information possesses which of the following characteristics?

a. Timeliness
b. Conservatism
c. Materiality
d. Comparability

Financial Statement Formats

First, let's
look at the
asset section
of a classified
balance
sheet.

Polly's Place, Inc.
Balance Sheet
December 31, 1998

ASSETS	
Current assets:	
Cash and cash equivalents	$ 58,000
Accounts receivable, net	9,500
Inventories, net	33,000
Deferred taxes	6,000
Other current assets	3,000
Total current assets	109,500
Property, plant and equipment, net	16,000
Other assets	15,000
Total assets	$140,500

Polly's Place, Inc.
Balance Sheet
December 31, 1998

ASSETS
Current assets:
Cash and cash equivalents
Accounts receivable, net
Inventories, net
Deferred taxes
Other current assets
Total current assets
Property, plant and equipment,
Other assets
Total assets

Current assets are assets that will be turned into cash or expire (be used up) within the longer of one year or the operating cycle.

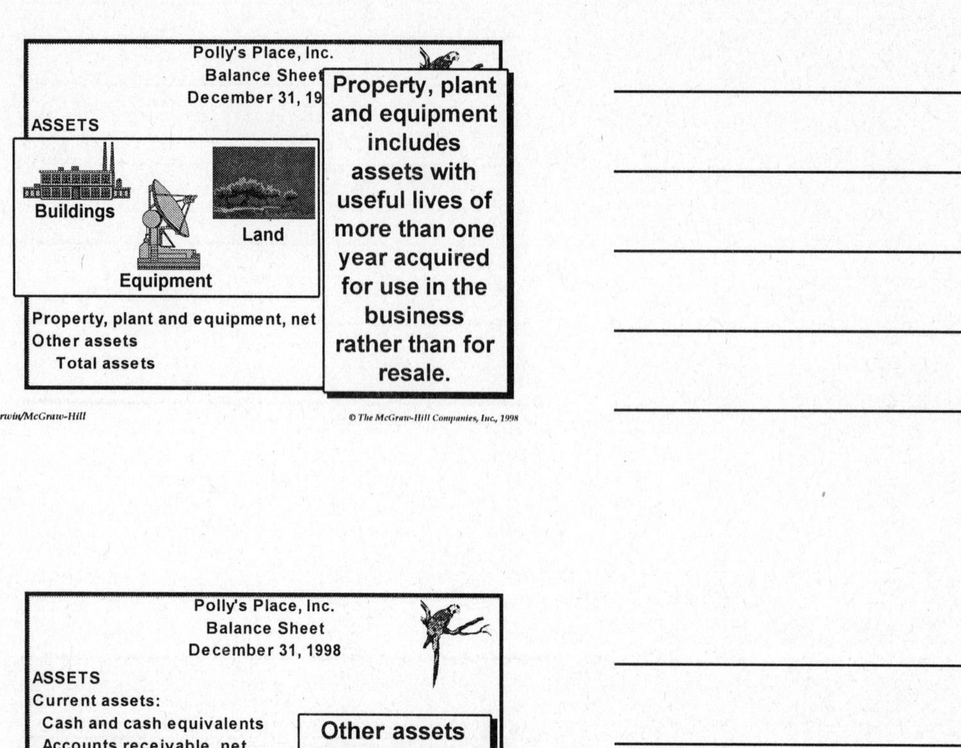

Irwin/McGraw-Hill

Property, plant and equipment includes assets with useful lives of more than one year acquired for use in the business rather than for resale.

Polly's Place, Inc.
Balance Sheet
December 31, 1998

ASSETS
Current assets:
Cash and cash equivalents
Accounts receivable, net
Inventories, net
Deferred taxes
Other current assets
Total current assets
Property, plant and equipment, n
Other assets
Total assets

Other assets may include intangible assets such as patents, goodwill, copyrights, etc.

Irwin/McGraw-Hill

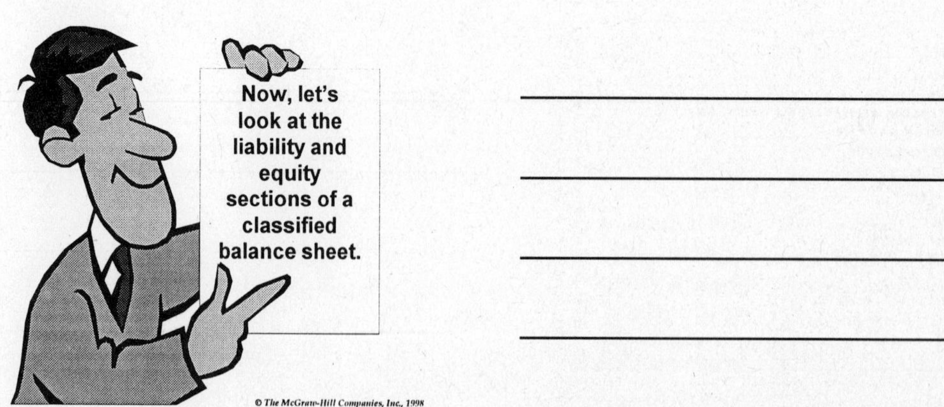

Now, let's look at the liability and equity sections of a classified balance sheet.

Irwin/McGraw-Hill

Polly's Place, Inc.
Balance Sheet
December 31, 1998

LIABILITIES AND STOCKHOLDERS' EQUITY	
Current liabilities:	
Accounts payable and accrued expenses	$ 8,000
Accrued wages payable	9,000
Income taxes payable	3,000
Total current liabilities	20,000
Long-term debt	8,000
Total liabilities	28,000
Stockholders' equity:	
Common stock, $.01 par value, 90,000 share authorized, 5,000 issued and outstanding	100
Paid-in capital	60,000
Retained earnings	52,400
Total stockholders' equity	112,500
Total liabilities and stockholders' equity	$140,500

Irwin/McGraw-Hill

Polly's Place, Inc.
Balance Sheet
December 31, 1998

LIABILITIES AND STOCKHOLDERS' EQUITY	
Current liabilities:	
Accounts payable and accrued expenses	$ 8,000
Accrued wages payable	9,000
Income taxes payable	3,000
Total current liabilities	20,000
Paid-in capital	60,000
Retained earnings	52,400
Total stockholders' equity	112,500
Total liabilities and stockholders' equity	$140,500

Current liabilities are obligations that will be paid with current assets, normally within one year.

Irwin/McGraw-Hill

Polly's Place, Inc.
Balance Sheet
December 31, 1998

LIABILITIES AND STOCKHOLDERS' EQUITY	
Current liabilities:	
Accounts payable and accrued expenses	$ 8,000
Accrued wages payable	9,000
Income taxes payable	3,000
Total current liabilities	20,000
Long-term debt	8,000
Total liabilities	28,000
Total liabilities and stockholders' equity	$140,500

Long-term liabilities are debts that have maturity dates extending beyond one year from the balance sheet date.

Irwin/McGraw-Hill

Polly's Place, Inc.

Contributed capital is often shown in two separate accounts.

❶**Common stock** - represents the par value of the stock that has been sold.

❷**Paid-in capital in excess of par** - represents the amount received above the par value.

Total liabilities	28,000
Stockholders' equity:	
Common stock, $.01 par value, 90,000 share authorized, 5,000 issued and outstanding	100
Paid-in capital	60,000
Retained earnings	52,400
Total stockholders' equity	112,500
Total liabilities and stockholders' equity	$140,500

Polly's Place, Inc.
Balance Sheet
December 31, 1998

LIABILITIES AND STOCKHOLDERS' EQUITY

Current liabilities:	
Accounts payable and accrued expenses	$ 8,000
Accrued wages payable	9,000

Retained earnings is the accumulated earnings of the company less the accumulated dividends declared.

Stockholders' equity:	
Common stock, $.01 par value, 90,000 share authorized, 5,000 issued and outstanding	100
Paid-in capital	60,000
Retained earnings	52,400
Total stockholders' equity	112,500
Total liabilities and stockholders' equity	$140,500

Irwin/McGraw-Hill © The McGraw-Hill Companies, Inc, 1998

I see! They equal!

A = L + SE

140,500 = 28,000 + 112,500

Irwin/McGraw-Hill © The McGraw-Hill Companies, Inc, 1998

Par Value

Par Value

Nominal value

Established by board of directors

Par Value ≠ Market Value

10000 25,509,000

Contributed Capital Example

On May 1, Molly's Mart, Inc. sold 1,000,000 shares of its $.01 par value common stock for $25.50 per share.

Prepare the journal entry.

Page 34

Date		Description	Post. Ref.	Debit	Credit

Liquidity

Liquidity refers to a company's ability to meet its current maturing debts.

Tests of liquidity include:

Current Assets	
-	Current Liabilities
	Working Capital

Current Assets	
÷	Current Liabilities
	Current Ratio

Debt Contracts

When companies enter into a debt contract, they often agree to specific restrictions to protect the creditors.

Examples include maintaining a specified cash balance or current ratio.

Classified Income Statement

Income statements have up to five major sections:

❶Continuing operations
❷Discontinued operations
❸Extraordinary items
❹Cumulative effect of changes in accounting methods
❺Earnings per share

Classified Income Statement

Can you find the following sections on the income statement on the next screen?

Continuing operations

Extraordinary items

Earnings per share

Polly's Place, Inc. Income Statement For Year Ended December 31, 1998	
Net sales	$ 447,500
Cost of goods sold	341,100
Gross profit	106,400
Selling expenses	23,950
General and administrative expenses	27,300
Income from operations	55,150
Other income (expense)	
Interest income (expense), net	950
Income before income taxes	56,100
Provision for income taxes	11,220
Income before extraordinary item	44,880
Loss from earthquake (net of $1,000 tax benefit)	(4,000)
Net Income	$ 40,880
Earnings per share (5,000 shares outstanding)	
Income before extraordinary item	$ 8.98
Extraordinary item	(0.80)
Net income	$ 8.18

Continuing Operations

Now, let's look at three common formats for presenting the continuing operations section.

1. Single-step
2. Multiple-step (one subtotal)
3. Multiple-step (two subtotals)

Single-Step Income Statement

Polly's Place, Inc. Income Statement For Year Ended December 31, 1998		
Net sales		$ 447,500
Interest income, net		950
Total revenues		448,450
Cost of goods sold	$341,100	
Selling expenses	23,950	
General and admn. exp.	27,300	
Total operating expenses		392,350
Income before income taxes		56,100
Provision for income taxes		11,220
Income before extraordinary item		44,880
Loss from earthquake (net of $1,000 tax benefit)		(4,000)
Net Income		$ 40,880

Multiple-Step (One Subtotal)

Polly's Place, Inc.
Income Statement
For Year Ended December 31, 1998

Net sales	$ 447,500
Cost of goods sold	341,100
Selling expenses	23,950
General and administrative expenses	27,300
Income from operations	55,150
Other income (expense)	
Interest income (expense), net	950
Income before income taxes	56,100
Provision for income taxes	11,220
Income before extraordinary item	44,880
Loss from earthquake (net of $1,000	(4,000)
Net Income	$ 40,880

One subtotal for income from operations is presented.

Irwin/McGraw-Hill

Multiple-Step (Two Subtotals)

Polly's Place, Inc.
Income Statement
For Year Ended December 31, 1998

Net sales	$ 447,500
Cost of goods sold	341,100
Gross profit	106,400
Selling expenses	23,950
General and administrative expenses	27,300
Income from operations	55,150
Other income (expense)	
Interest income (expense), net	950
Income before income taxes	56,100
Provision for income taxes	11,220
Income before extraordinary item	44,880
Loss from earthquake (net of $1,00(	(4,000)
Net Income	$ 40,880

Two subtotals are presented: gross profit and income from operations.

Irwin/McGraw-Hill

Multiple-Step (Two Subtotals)

Polly's Place, Inc.
Income Statement
For Year Ended December 31, 1998

Net sales	$ 447,500
Cost of goods sold	341,100
Gross profit	106,400
Selling expenses	23,950
General and administrative	27,300
Income from operations	55,150
Other income (expense)	
Interest income (expense),	950
Income before income taxe	56,100
Provision for income taxes	11,220
Income before extraordinary item	44,880
Loss from earthquake (net of $1,000 tax benefit)	(4,000)
Net Income	$ 40,880

Net sales are gross sales minus any discounts, returns, and allowances during the period.

Irwin/McGraw-Hill

Multiple-Step (Two Subtotals)

Polly's Place, Inc.
Income Statement
For Year Ended December 31, 1998

Net sales	$ 447,500
Cost of goods sold	341,100
Gross profit	106,400
Selling expenses	23,950
General and administrative	27,300
Income from operations	55,150
Other income (expense)	
Interest income (expense),	950
Income before income taxe	56,100
Provision for income taxes	11,220
Income before extraordinary item	44,880
Loss from earthquake (net of $1,000 tax benefit)	(4,000)
Net Income	$ 40,880

Cost of goods sold is the cost of inventory sold by a merchandiser or a manufacturer during the period.

Multiple-Step (Two Subtotals)

Polly's Place, Inc.
Income Statement
For Year Ended December 31, 1998

Net sales	$ 447,500
Cost of goods sold	341,100
Gross profit	106,400
Selling expenses	23,950
General and administrative e	27,300
Income from operations	55,150
Other income (expense)	
Interest income (expense),	950
Income before income taxes	56,100
Provision for income taxes	11,220
Income before extraordinary item	44,880
Loss from earthquake (net of $1,000 tax benefit)	(4,000)
Net Income	$ 40,880

Gross profit is a subtotal not an account.

Multiple-Step (Two Subtotals)

Polly's Place, Inc.
Income Statement
For Year Ended December 31, 1998

Net sales	$ 447,500
Cost of goods sold	341,100
Gross profit	106,400
Selling expenses	23,950
General and administrative	27,300
Income from operations	55,150
Other income (expense)	
Interest income (expense)	950
Income before income taxe	56,100
Provision for income taxes	11,220
Income before extraordinary item	44,880
Loss from earthquake (net of $1,000 tax benefit)	(4,000)
Net Income	$ 40,880

Gross profit percentage is calculated as:

Gross profit ÷ Net sales

$106,400 ÷ $447,500 = 23.78%

Multiple-Step (Two Subtotals)

Polly's Place, Inc.
Income Statement
For Year Ended December 31, 1998

Net sales	$ 447,500
Cost of goods sold	341,100
Gross profit	106,400
Selling expenses	23,950
General and administrative expenses	27,300
Income from operations	55,150
Other i	
Intere	950
Income	56,100
Provisi	11,220
Income	44,880
Loss f	(4,000)
Net Inc	40,880

Operating expenses:

Selling expenses include all amounts incurred related to sales activities.

General and administrative expenses include all amounts incurred for the overall business.

Multiple-Step (Two Subtotals)

Polly's Place, Inc.
Income Statement
For Year Ended December 31, 1998

Net sales	$ 447,500
Cost of goods sold	341,100
Gross profit	106,400
Selling expenses	23,950
General and administrative expenses	27,300
Income from operations	55,150
Other income (expense)	
Intere	950
Income	56,100
Provisi	11,220
Income	44,880
Loss from earthquake (net of $1,000 tax benefit)	(4,000)
Net Income	$ 40,880

Income from operations is a subtotal that is computed as gross profit minus operating expenses.

Multiple-Step (Two Subtotals)

Polly's Place, Inc.
Income Statement

Net sale	447,500
Cost of	341,100
Gross	106,400
Selling	23,950
General	27,300
Income from operations	55,150
Other income (expense)	
Interest income (expense), net	950
Income before income taxes	56,100
Provision for income taxes	11,220
Income before extraordinary item	44,880
Loss from earthquake (net of $1,000 tax benefit)	(4,000)
Net Income	$ 40,880

Other income (expense) includes nonoperating items such as interest income and expense, gains and losses on the sale of assets, and dividend revenue.

Multiple-Step (Two Subtotals)

Polly's Place, Inc.
Income Statement
For Year Ended December 31, 1998

> The nonoperating items are added to or subtracted from income from operations to obtain income before income taxes (pretax earnings).

Net sal	447,500
Cost of	341,100
Gross	106,400
Selling	23,950
Genera	27,300
Income from operations	55,150
Other income (expense)	
Interest income (expense), net	950
Income before income taxes	56,100
Provision for income taxes	11,220
Income before extraordinary item	44,880
Loss from earthquake (net of $1,000 tax benefit)	(4,000)
Net Income	$ 40,880

Multiple-Step (Two Subtotals)

Polly's Place, Inc.
Income Statement
For Year Ended December 31, 1998

> The provision for income taxes represents the tax expense related to the continuing operations of the company.

Net sales	$ 447,500
Cost of goods sold	341,100
Gross profit	106,400
Selling	23,950
Genera	27,300
Incom	55,150
Other i	
Interest income (expense), net	950
Income before income taxes	56,100
Provision for income taxes	11,220
Income before extraordinary item	44,880
Loss from earthquake (net of $1,000 tax benefit)	(4,000)
Net Income	$ 40,880

Classified Income Statement

Now that we have discussed the continuing operations section, let's discuss the other major sections of the income statement.

Discontinued Operations

Sale or abandonment of a segment of a business.

Income or loss on segment's operation for the period.

Gain or loss on disposal of the segment.

Show net of tax effect.

Extraordinary Items

Unusual

Infrequent

Show net of tax effect.

Cumulative Effect of Changes in Accounting Methods

GAAP Method — Change to Alternative → GAAP Method

Changes must be to a preferable method and must be disclosed in notes to financial statements.

Show net of tax effect.

Earnings Per Share

$$\frac{\text{Net income available to common shareholders}}{\text{Weighted-average number of common shares outstanding}}$$

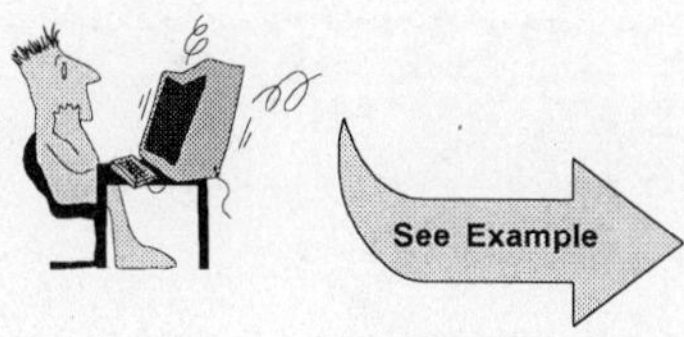

See Example

Polly's Place, Inc.
Income Statement
For Year Ended December 31, 1998

Net sales	$ 447,500
Cost of goods sold	341,100
Gross profit	$ 106,400
Selling expenses	23,950
General and administrative expenses	27,300
Income from operations	55,150
Other income (expense)	
Interest income (expense), net	950
Income before income taxes	56,100
Provision for income taxes	11,220
Income before extraordinary item	44,880
Loss from earthquake (net of $1,000 tax benefit)	(4,000)
Net Income	40,880
Earnings per share (5,000 shares outstanding)	
Income before extraordinary item	$ 8.98
Extraordinary item	(0.80)
Net income	$ 8.18

Polly's Place, Inc.
Statement of Cash Flows
For Year Ended December 31, 1998

Cash flows from operating activities:		
Net income	$ 40,880	
Adjustments to net income:		
Depreciation	2,000	
Loss from earthquake	4,000	
Increase (decrease) in cash from changes in:		
Accounts receivable, net	1,500	
Inventories, net	(12,000)	
Deferred taxes	(3,000)	
Other assets	(1,500)	
Accounts payable and accrued expenses	3,000	
Accrued wages payable	1,500	
Income taxes payable	(500)	
Net cash provided by operating activities		$ 35,880

Continued . . .

Polly's Place, Inc.
Statement of Cash Flows
For Year Ended December 31, 1998

Cash flows from investing activites:		
Capital expenditures	(10,000)	
Sale of fixed assets	500	
Purchase of other assets	(2,500)	
Net cash used by investing activities		(12,000)
Cash flows from financing activities:		
Issuance of common stock	50	
Dividends paid, net	(18,000)	
Net cash used by financing activities		(17,950)
Net increase in cash and cash equivalents		5,930
Cash and cash equivalents at beginning of year		52,070
Cash and cash equivalents at end of year		$ 58,000

Now, let's look at the whole statement . . .

Polly's Place, Inc.
Statement of Cash Flows
For Year Ended December 31, 1998

Cash flows from operating activities:		
Net income	$ 40,880	
Adjustments to net income:		
Depreciation	2,000	
Loss from earthquake	4,000	
Increase (decrease) in cash from changes in:		
Accounts receivable, net	1,500	
Inventories, net	(12,000)	
Deferred taxes	(3,000)	
Other assets	(1,500)	
Accounts payable and accrued expenses	3,000	
Accrued wages payable	1,500	
Income taxes payable	(500)	
Net cash provided by operating activities		$ 35,880
Cash flows from investing activites:		
Capital expenditures	(10,000)	
Sale of fixed assets	500	
Purchase of other assets	(2,500)	
Net cash used by investing activities		(12,000)
Cash flows from financing activities:		
Issuance of common stock	50	
Dividends paid, net	(18,000)	
Net cash used by financing activities		(17,950)
Net increase in cash and cash equivalents		5,930
Cash and cash equivalents at beginning of year		52,070
Cash and cash equivalents at end of year		$ 58,000

Irwin/McGraw-Hill

© The McGraw-Hill Companies, Inc., 1998

Notes to Financial Statements

Significant accounting policies used by the company

Additional detail concerning the data shown on the financial statements

Other relevant financial information concerning pension funds, stock options, subsequent events, etc.

Disclosure Process

Press releases

Annual reports

Quarterly reports

SEC reports: 10-K, 10-Q, 8-K

The End of Chapter 5

Maybe I should issue a press release to disclose my identity!

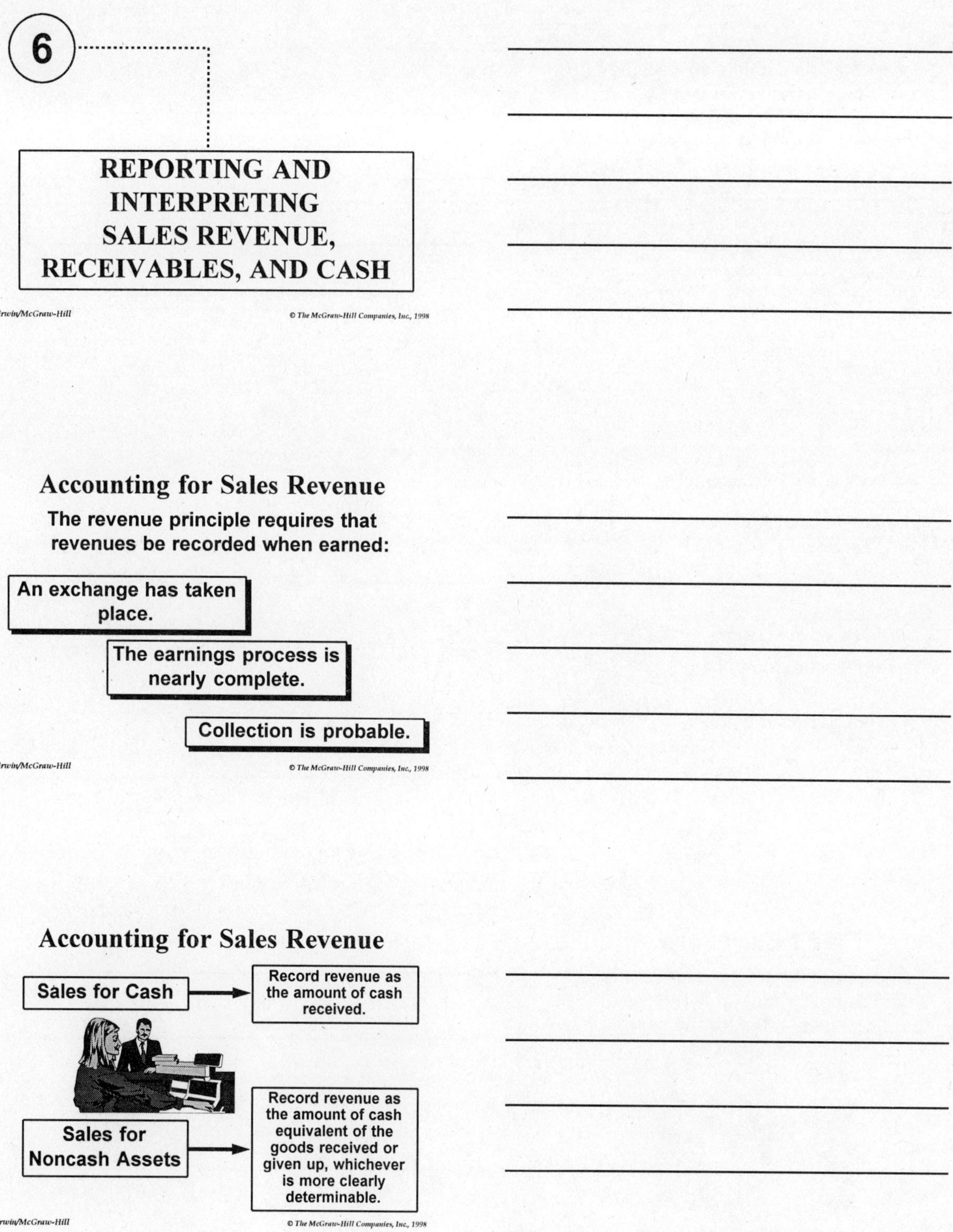
6
REPORTING AND INTERPRETING SALES REVENUE, RECEIVABLES, AND CASH
Irwin/McGraw-Hill
© The McGraw-Hill Companies, Inc., 1998
Accounting for Sales Revenue
The revenue principle requires that revenues be recorded when earned:
An exchange has taken place.
The earnings process is nearly complete.
Collection is probable.
Irwin/McGraw-Hill
© The McGraw-Hill Companies, Inc., 1998
Accounting for Sales Revenue
Sales for Cash
Record revenue as the amount of cash received.
Sales for Noncash Assets
Record revenue as the amount of cash equivalent of the goods received or given up, whichever is more clearly determinable.
Irwin/McGraw-Hill
© The McGraw-Hill Companies, Inc., 1998

Cash Sales

On July 6, Kid's Clothes sold $550 of merchandise for cash.

Prepare the journal entry.

GENERAL JOURNAL					Page 34
Date		Description	Post. Ref.	Debit	Credit

Credit Card Sales

Companies accept credit cards for several reasons:

To increase sales.

To avoid providing credit directly to customers.

To avoid losses due to bad checks.

To receive payment quicker.

Credit Card Sales

When credit card sales are made, the company must pay the credit card company a fee for the service it provides.

Credit Card Sales

On July 6, Kid's Clothes' credit card sales were $1,500. The credit card company charges a 2% service fee.

Prepare the journal entry.

Credit Card Discounts may be reported as a contra revenue account or as a selling expense.

Date		Description	Post. Ref.	Debit	Credit

Credit Sales

When companies allow customers to purchase merchandise on an open account, the customer promises to pay the company in the future for the purchase.

Credit Sales

On July 6, Kid's Clothes sold $300 of merchandise on account.

Prepare the journal entry.

GENERAL JOURNAL **Page 34**

Date		Description	Post. Ref.	Debit	Credit

Credit Sales and Sales Discounts

When customers purchase on open account, they may be offered a sales discount to encourage early payment.

2/10, n/30

Read as: "Two ten, net thirty"

Credit Sales and Sales Discounts

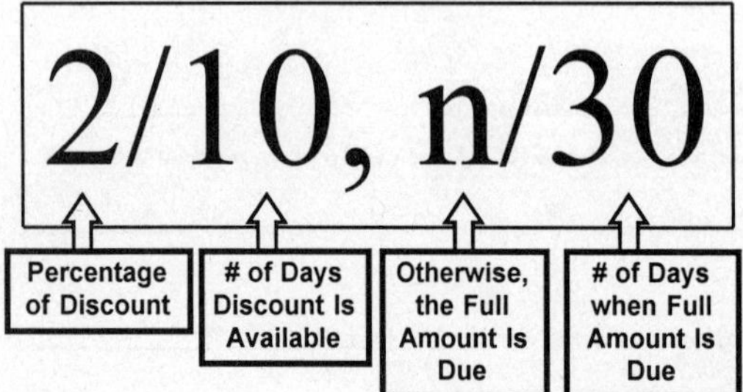

| Percentage of Discount | # of Days Discount Is Available | Otherwise, the Full Amount Is Due | # of Days when Full Amount Is Due |

Credit Sales and Sales Discounts

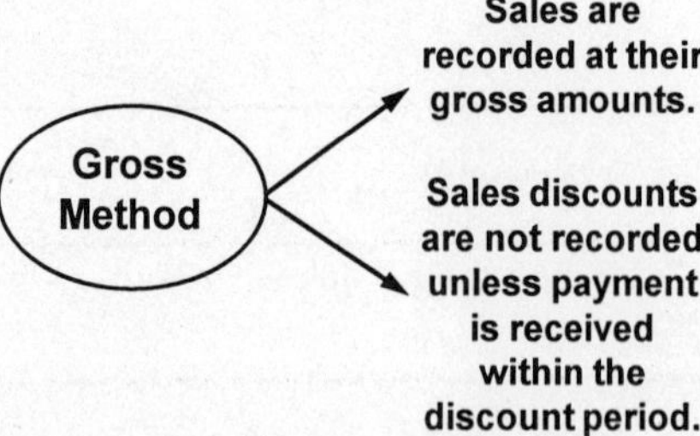

Gross Method
Sales are recorded at their gross amounts.
Sales discounts are not recorded unless payment is received within the discount period.

Credit Sales and Sales Discounts

On July 6, Kid's Clothes sold $400 of merchandise on credit with terms of 2/10, n/30.

Prepare the journal entry.

GENERAL JOURNAL — Page 34

Date		Description	Post. Ref.	Debit	Credit

Credit Sales and Sales Discounts

On July 14, Kid's Clothes receives the appropriate payment from the customer for the July 6 sale.

Prepare the journal entry.

Sales Discounts may be reported as a contra revenue account or as a selling expense.

Page 34

Date		Description	Post. Ref.	Debit	Credit

Credit Sales and Sales Discounts

If the customer remits the appropriate amount on July 20, what entry would Kid's Clothes make?

Since the customer paid outside of the discount period, a sales discount is not granted.

34

Date		Description	Ref.	Debit	Credit

Sales Returns and Allowances

Debited for damaged merchandise.

Debited for returned merchandise.

Contra revenue account.

Sales Returns and Allowances

On July 8, a customer returns $25 of damaged merchandise that was originally purchased for cash to Kid's Clothes.

Prepare the journal entry.

GENERAL JOURNAL — Page 34

Date		Description	Post. Ref.	Debit	Credit

Reporting Net Sales

Companies account for sales discounts, sales returns and allowances, and credit card discounts separately to allow management monitoring of these transactions.

Reporting Net Sales

Sales revenue	
Less:	Sales returns and allowances
	Sales discounts
	Credit card discounts
Net sales	

Measuring and Reporting Receivables

Accounts Receivable

- Claims against other companies or persons for cash, goods, or services.
- Open accounts owed to the business by trade customers.

Measuring and Reporting Receivables

$1200 Wheaton, Ohio January 5, 1999

Sixty days after date I promise to pay to

the order of Wheaton Mountain Bank

One thousand two hundred ------------------------------ Dollars

Payable at Wheaton Mountain Bank

Value received with interest at 12% per annum

No. 10242 Due March 6, 1999 *Pat Rogers*

Kid's Clothes

Measuring and Reporting Receivables

$1200 Wheaton, Ohio January 5, 1999

Sixty days after date I promise to pay to

the Wheaton Mountain Bank

One thousand two hundred ------------------------------ Dollars

Payable at Wheaton Mountain Bank

Value received with interest at 12% per annum

No. 10242 Due March 6, 1999 Pat Rogers

Kid's Clothes

Accounting for Bad Debts

Bad debts result from credit customers who will not pay the business the amount they owe, regardless of collection efforts.

Accounting for Bad Debts

Accounting for Bad Debts

Most businesses record an estimate of the bad debt expense by an adjusting entry at the end of the accounting period.

Recording Bad Debt Expense Estimates

Kid's Clothes estimated bad debt expense for 1998 to be $1,500.

Prepare the adjusting entry.

The Allowance for Doubtful Accounts is a contra asset account.

Date					Page 78 Credit

Allowance for Doubtful Accounts

Accounts receivable
Less: Allowance for doubtful accounts
Net realizable value of accounts receivable

The net realizable value is the amount of accounts receivable that the business expects to collect.

Writing Off Uncollectible Accounts

When it is clear that a specific customer's account receivable will be uncollectible, the amount should be removed from the Accounts Receivable account and charged to the Allowance for Doubtful Accounts.

Writing Off Uncollectible Accounts

Assume that on January 5, Kid's Clothes determined that Jason Clark would not pay the $500 he owes.

Prepare the journal entry.

GENERAL JOURNAL					Page 1
Date		Description	Post. Ref.	Debit	Credit

Writing Off Uncollectible Accounts

Assume that before this entry, the Accounts Receivable balance was $10,000 and the Allowance for Doubtful Accounts balance was $2,500.

Let's see what effect the write-off had on these accounts.

Writing Off Uncollectible Accounts

	Before Write-Off	After Write-Off
Accounts receivable	$10,000	$ 9,500
Less: Allow. for doubtful accts.	2,500	2,000
Net realizable value	$ 7,500	$ 7,500

Notice that the $500 write-off did not change the net realizable value nor did it affect any income statement accounts.

Reinstatement of Accounts Written Off

When a customer makes a payment after an account has been written off, two journal entries are required:

➊ Reverse the write-off.

➋ Record the cash collection.

Reinstatement of Accounts Written Off

Assume that on January 30, Jason Clark surprised Kid's Clothes by paying $500 he owed.

➊ Reverse the write-off.

GENERAL JOURNAL Page 10

Date		Description	Post. Ref.	Debit	Credit

Reinstatement of Accounts Written Off

Assume that on January 30, Jason Clark surprised Kid's Clothes by paying $500 he owed.

❷ Record the cash collection.

GENERAL JOURNAL — Page 10

Date		Description	Post. Ref.	Debit	Credit

Estimating Bad Debts

How do we estimate the amount of the bad debts at the end of the accounting period?

Methods for Estimating Bad Debts

Percentage of credit sales

or

Aging of accounts receivable

Percentage of Credit Sales

Bad debt percentage is based on actual uncollectible accounts from prior years' credit sales.

Focus is on determining the amount to record on the income statement as Bad Debt Expense.

Percentage of Credit Sales

Net Credit Sales
× % Estimated Uncollectible
Amount of Journal Entry

Percentage of Credit Sales

In 1997, Kid's Clothes had credit sales of $50,000 and $500 of these sales ultimately became uncollectible.

What percentage of the credit sales was uncollected?

Percentage of Credit Sales

Now, in 1998, Kid's Clothes had credit sales of $60,000.

Using the 1997 percentage of 1%, what is the estimate of bad debts expense for 1998?

Irwin/McGraw-Hill

Percentage of Credit Sales

GENERAL JOURNAL					Page 76
Date		Description	Post. Ref.	Debit	Credit

Irwin/McGraw-Hill

Irwin/McGraw-Hill

Aging of Accounts Receivable

Focus is on determining the desired balance in the Allowance for Doubtful Accounts on the balance sheet.

Aging of Accounts Receivable

	Accounts Receivable
×	% Estimated Uncollectible
	Desired Balance in Allowance Account
-	Allowance Account Credit Balance
	Amount of Journal Entry

	Accounts Receivable
×	% Estimated Uncollectible
	Desired Balance in Allowance Account
+	Allowance Account Debit Balance
	Amount of Journal Entry

Aging Schedule

Each customer's account is aged by breaking down the balance by showing the age (in number of days) of each part of the balance.

An aging of accounts receivable for Kid's Clothes in 1998 might look like this . . .

Aging Schedule

Customer	Not Yet Due	Days Past Due 1-30	31-60	61-90	Over 90	Total A/R Balance
Aaron, R.		$ 235				$ 235
Baxter, T.	$1,200	300				1,500
Clark, J.			$ 50	$ 200	$ 500	750
Zak, R.			325			325
Total	$3,500	$2,550	$1,830	$1,540	$1,240	$10,660

Based on past experience, the business estimates the percentage of uncollectible accounts in each time category.

Irwin/McGraw-Hill

Aging Schedule

Customer	Not Yet Due	Days Past Due 1-30	31-60	61-90	Over 90	Total A/R Balance
Aaron, R.		$ 235				$ 235
Baxter, T.	$1,200	300				1,500
Clark, J.			$ 50	$ 200	$ 500	750
Zak, R.			325			325
Total	$3,500	$2,550	$1,830	$1,540	$1,240	$10,660
% Uncollectible	0.01	0.04	0.10	0.25	0.40	

These percentages are then multiplied by the appropriate column totals.

Irwin/McGraw-Hill

Aging Schedule

The column totals are then added to arrive at the total estimate of uncollectible accounts.

Customer	Not Yet Due	Days Past Due 1-30	31-60	61-90	Over 90	Total A/R Balance
Aaron,						235
Baxter						1,500
Clark, J.			$ 50	$ 200	$ 500	750
Zak, R.			325			325
Total	$3,500	$2,550	$1,830	$1,540	$1,240	$10,660
% Uncollectible	0.01	0.04	0.10	0.25	0.40	
Estimated Uncoll. Amount	$ 35	$ 102	$ 183	$ 385	$ 496	

Irwin/McGraw-Hill

Aging Schedule

Custom		Days Past Due				Total A/R Balance
Aaron,						235
Baxter,						1,500
Clark,						750
Zak, R.			325			325
Total	$3,500	$2,550	$1,830	$1,540	$1,240	$10,660
% Uncollectible	0.01	0.04	0.10	0.25	0.40	
Estimated Uncoll. Amount	$ 35	$ 102	$ 183	$ 385	$ 496	$ 1,201

The total estimated amount ($1,201) is the balance that we want in the Allowance for Doubtful Accounts at the end of the period.

Irwin/McGraw-Hill

Aging of Accounts Receivable

Custome		Days Past Due				Total A/R Balance
Aaron, R						235
Baxter,						1,500
Clark, J.						750
Zak, R.			325			325
Total	$3,500	$2,550	$1,830	$1,540	$1,240	$10,660
% Uncollectible	0.01	0.04	0.10	0.25	0.40	
Estimated Uncoll. Amount	$ 35	$ 102	$ 183	$ 385	$ 496	$ 1,201

Record the Dec. 31, 1998 adjusting entry assuming that the Allowance for Doubtful Accounts currently has a $50 credit balance.

Irwin/McGraw-Hill

Aging of Accounts Receivable

GENERAL JOURNAL — Page 76

Date		Description	Post. Ref.	Debit	Credit
Dec.	31	Bad Debt Expense		1,151	
		Allowance for Doubtful Accounts			1,151

	1,201	Desired Balance
-	50	Credit Balance
	$ 1,151	Adjusting Entry

After posting, the Allowance account would look like this . . .

Irwin/McGraw-Hill

Aging of Accounts Receivable

Allowance for Doubtful Accounts

	50	Balance at 12/31/98 before adj.
	1,151	1998 adjustment
	1,201	Balance at 12/31/98 after adj.

Notice that the balance after adjustment is equal to the estimate of $1,201 based on the aging analysis performed earlier.

Question

K-Stores estimates bad debts as 2% of credit sales.

The following information is available from K-Stores' Unadjusted Trial Balance:

Credit Sales	$120,000
Accounts Receivable	23,000
Allow. for Doubtful Accts.	450 (credit)

What is the amount of K-Stores' adjusting entry for Bad Debt Expense?

Question

GENERAL JOURNAL Page 76

Date		Description	Post. Ref.	Debit	Credit

Hey! We got that one . . . So let's try another one!

Question

K-Stores aged its accounts receivable and estimated that $2,400 would be uncollectible.

The following information is available from K-Stores' Unadjusted Trial Balance:

Credit Sales	$120,000	
Accounts Receivable	23,000	
Allow. for Doubtful Accts.	450	(credit)

How much would K-Stores adjust the Allowance for Doubtful Accounts?

Question

GENERAL JOURNAL					Page 76
Date		Description	Post. Ref.	Debit	Credit

Focus on Cash Flows

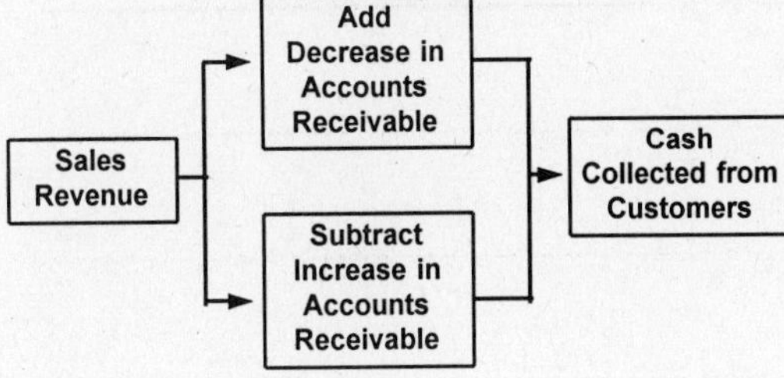

Irwin/McGraw-Hill

Cash and Cash Equivalents

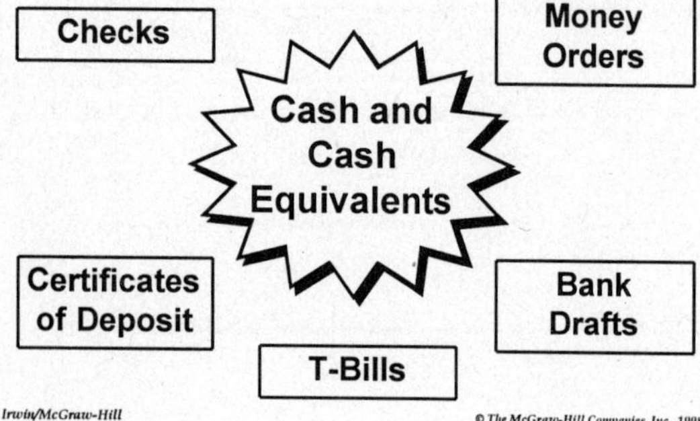

Irwin/McGraw-Hill

Internal Control of Cash

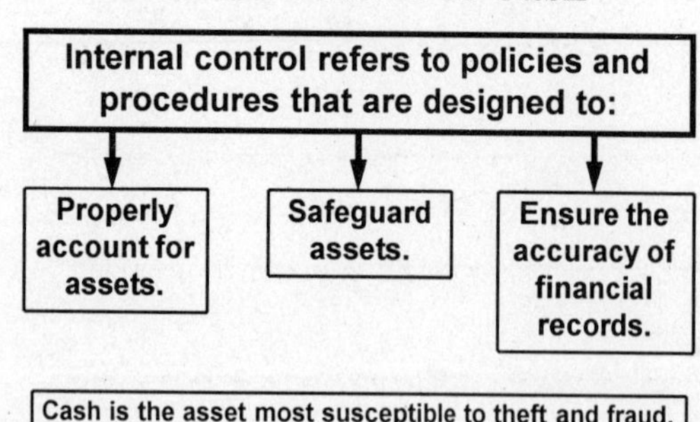

Irwin/McGraw-Hill

Internal Control of Cash

Separation of Duties → Custody, Recording, Authorization

Internal Control of Cash

Cash Controls:

- Bank Reconciliations
- Daily Deposits
- Prenumbered Checks
- Payment Approval
- Check Signatures
- Purchase Approval

Bank Reconciliation

Explains the difference between cash reported on bank statement and cash balance on company's books.

Provides information for reconciling journal entries.

Bank Reconciliation

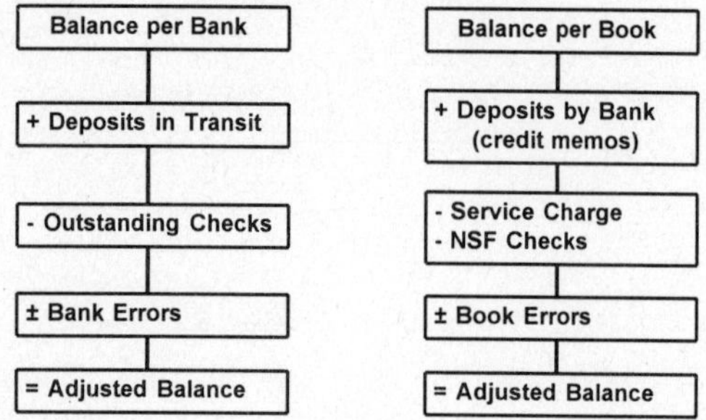

Irwin/McGraw-Hill

Bank Reconciliation

All reconciling items on the book side require an adjusting entry to the cash account.

Balance per Book
+ Deposits by Bank (credit memos)
- Service Charge
- NSF Checks
± Book Errors
= Adjusted Balance

Irwin/McGraw-Hill

Bank Reconciliation

Example

Prepare a July 31 bank reconciliation statement and the resulting journal entries for the Simmons Company. The July 31 bank statement indicated a cash balance of $9,610, while the cash ledger account on that date shows a balance of $7,430.

Additional information necessary for the reconciliation is shown on the next page.

Irwin/McGraw-Hill

Bank Reconciliation
Example

- Outstanding checks totaled $2,417.
- A $500 check mailed to the bank for deposit had not reached the bank at the statement date.
- The bank returned a customer's NSF check for $225 received as payment of an account receivable.
- The bank statement showed $30 interest earned on the bank balance for the month of July.
- Check 781 for supplies cleared the bank for $268 but was erroneously recorded in our books as $240.
- A $486 deposit by Acme Company was erroneously credited to our account by the bank.

Bank Reconciliation

Ending bank balance, July 31
Additions:
  Deposit in transit
Deductions:
  Bank error
  Outstanding checks
Correct cash balance

Ending book balance, July 31
Additions:
  Interest
Deductions:
  Recording error
  NSF check
Correct cash balance

Bank Reconciliation

GENERAL JOURNAL — Page 56

Date		Description	Post. Ref.	Debit	Credit

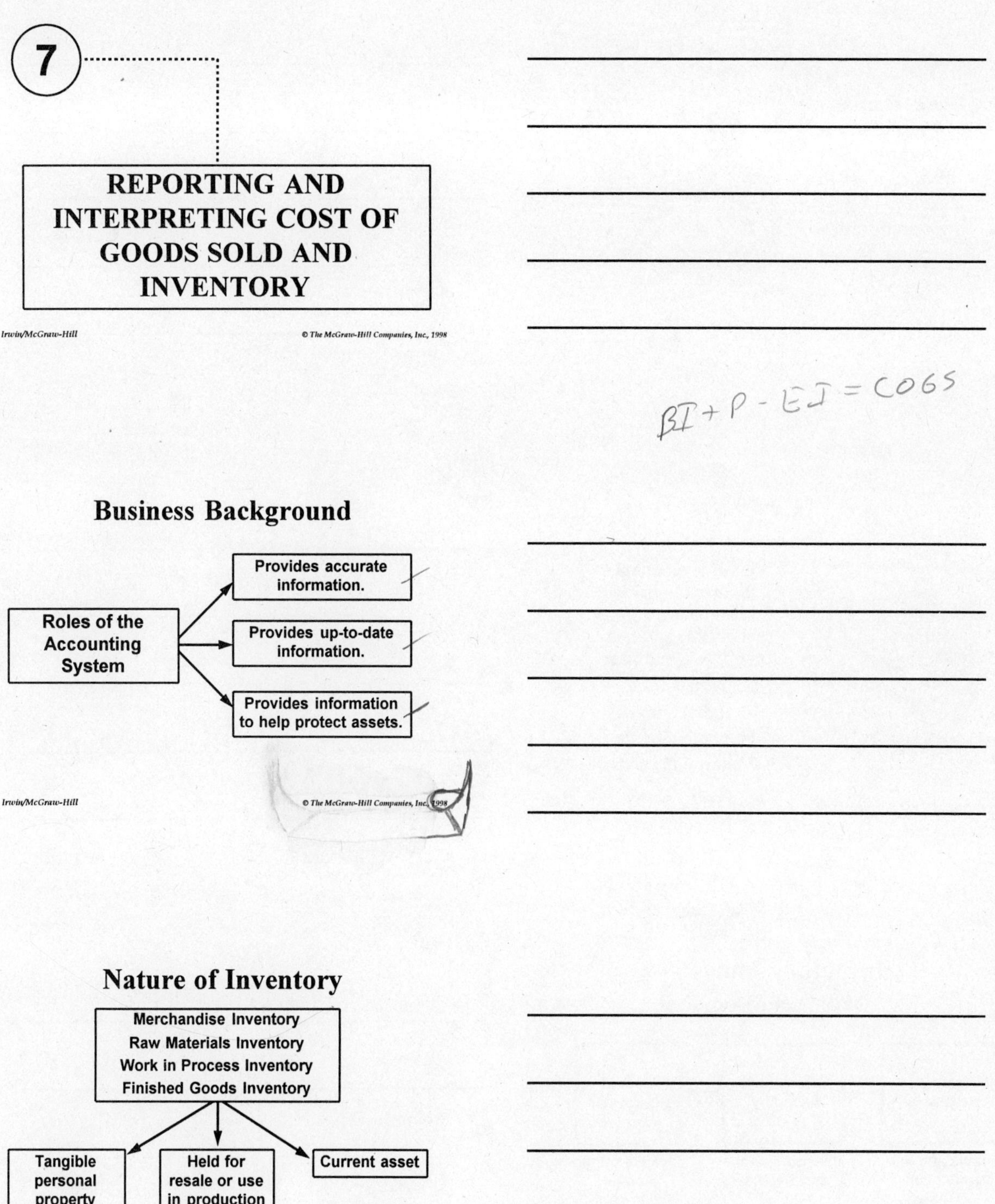

7
REPORTING AND INTERPRETING COST OF GOODS SOLD AND INVENTORY
Irwin/McGraw-Hill
© The McGraw-Hill Companies, Inc., 1998
Business Background
Roles of the Accounting System
Provides accurate information.
Provides up-to-date information.
Provides information to help protect assets.
Irwin/McGraw-Hill
© The McGraw-Hill Companies, Inc., 1998
Nature of Inventory
Merchandise Inventory
Raw Materials Inventory
Work in Process Inventory
Finished Goods Inventory
Tangible personal property
Held for resale or use in production of goods or services
Current asset
Irwin/McGraw-Hill
© The McGraw-Hill Companies, Inc., 1998

BI + P - EI = COGS

Inventory Cost

The cost principle requires that inventory be recorded at the price paid or the consideration given up.

Inventory Cost

Include all costs incurred to bring that asset to useable or saleable condition, such as:

Invoice price
Freight charges
Inspection costs
Preparation costs.

Inventory Flows
Merchandiser

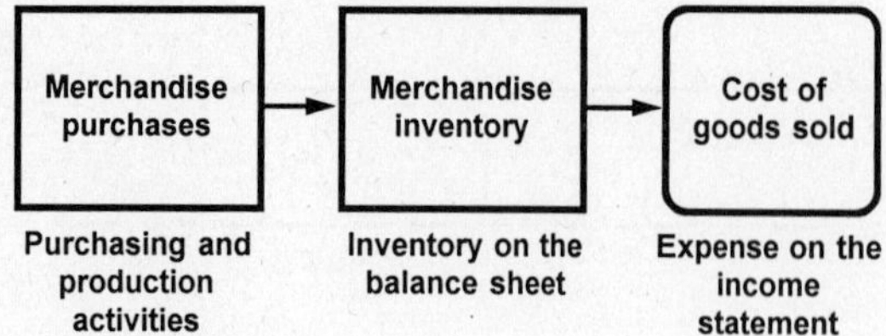

Inventory Flows
Manufacturer

Raw materials purchases → Raw materials inventory

Direct labor incurred

Factory overhead incurred

→ Work in process inventory

Purchasing and production activities

Inventory on the balance sheet

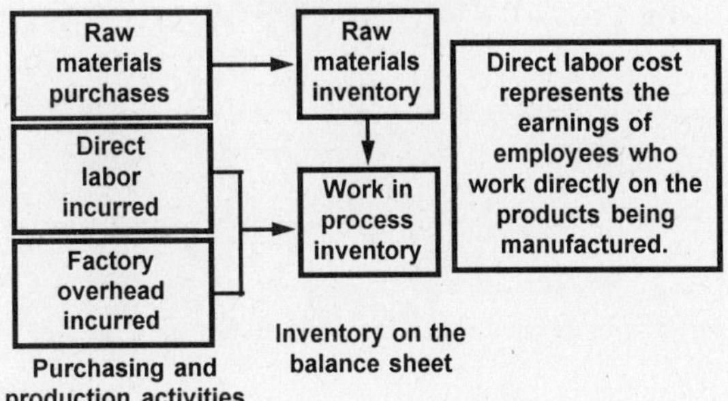

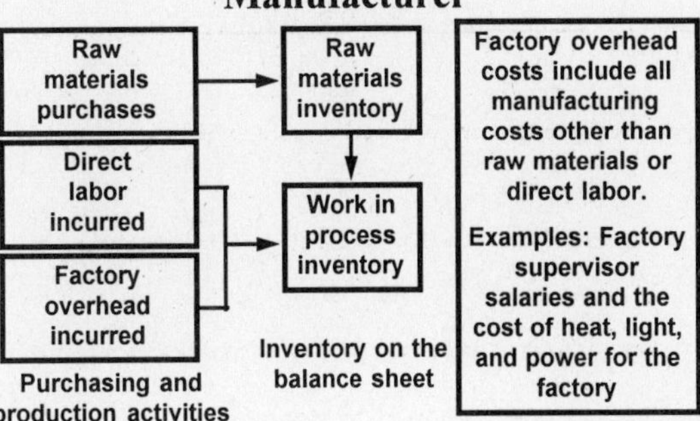

Inventory Flows
Manufacturer

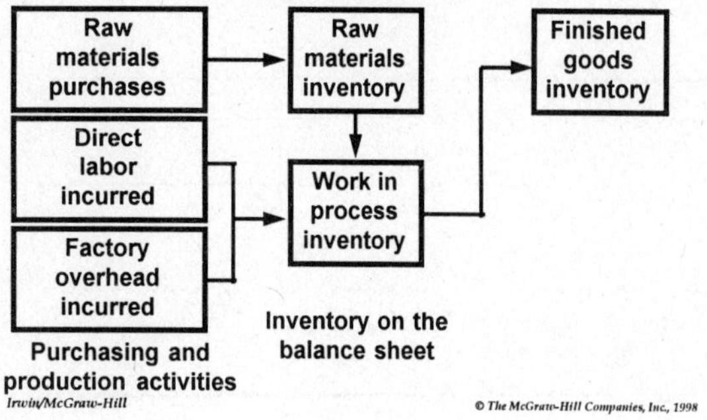

Inventory Flows
Manufacturer

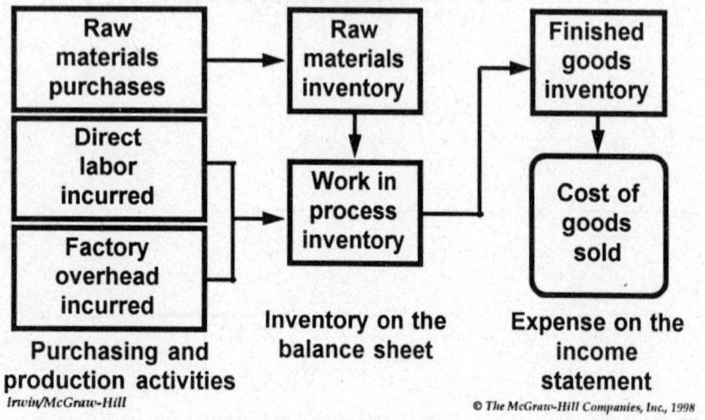

Cost of Goods Sold (CGS)

Number of units sold × unit costs = CGS

CGS is a major expense item for most nonservice businesses.

The measurement of CGS is an excellent example of the application of the matching principle.

Cost of Goods Sold (CGS)

Beginning inventory
Add: Purchases (net)
Goods available for sale
Deduct: Ending inventory
Cost of goods sold

Errors in Measuring Inventory

Errors in Measuring Inventory

	Beginning Inventory		Ending Inventory	
	Overstated	Understated	Overstated	Understated
Effect on Income Statement				
Goods Available for Sale	+	-	N/A	N/A
Cost of Goods Sold	+	-	-	+
Gross Profit	-	+	+	-
Net Income	-	+	+	-
Effect on Balance Sheet				
Inventory (12/31)	N/A	N/A	+	-
Retained Earnings	-	+	+	-

BI + P - EI = COGS

COGS ↑
BI ↑
NI ↓
G ↓

EI ↑
COGS ↓
NI ↑
G ↑

Gross Profit = Sales - COGS

Question

If the 1998 ending inventory is understated by $3,000, which of the following is true for 1998?

a. Beginning Inventory was understated.
b. Cost of Goods Sold will be understated.
c. Gross Profit will be overstated.
d. Net Income will be understated.

Question

If the 1998 ending inventory is understated by $3,000, which of the following is true for 1999?

a. Beginning Inventory was understated.
b. Cost of Goods Sold will be understated.
c. Gross Profit will be overstated.
d. All of the above.

Inventory Costing Methods

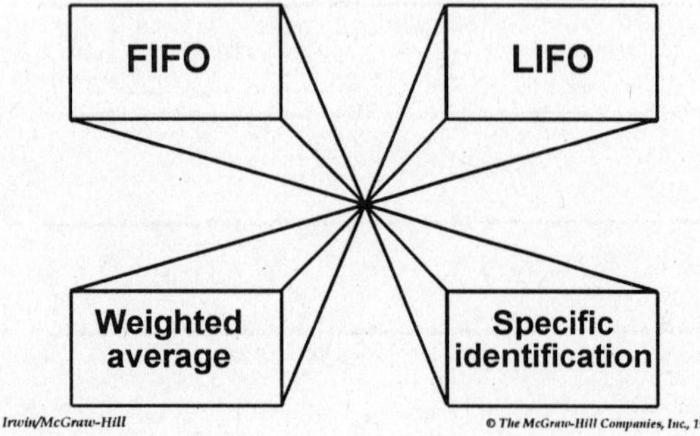

Inventory Costing Methods

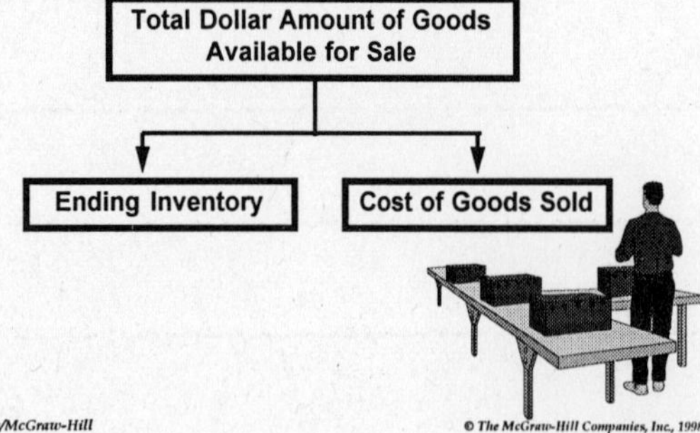

First-In, First-Out

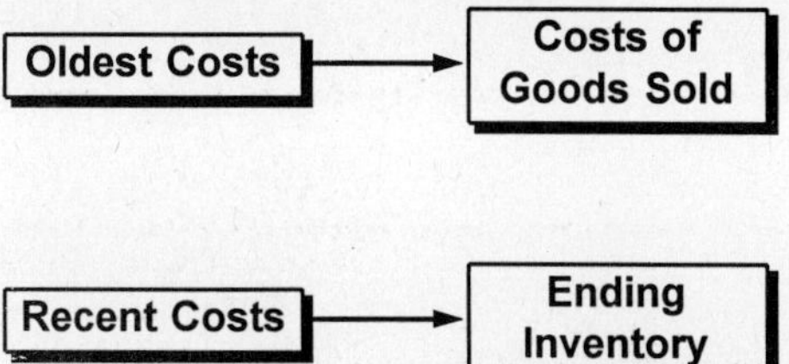

FIFO - Example

The schedule on the next screen shows the mouse pad inventory for Computers, Inc.

The physical inventory count shows 1,200 mouse pads in ending inventory.

Use the FIFO inventory method to determine:

(1) Ending inventory cost.

(2) Cost of goods sold.

FIFO - Example

Computers, Inc.
Mouse Pad Inventory

Date	Units	$/Unit	Total
Beginning Inventory	1,000	$ 5.25	$ 5,250.00
Purchases:			
Jan. 3	300	5.30	1,590.00
June 20	150	5.60	840.00
Sept. 15	200	5.80	1,160.00
Nov. 29	150	5.90	885.00
Goods Available for Sale	1,800		$ 9,725.00
Ending Inventory	1200		?
Cost of Goods Sold	600		?

FIFO - Example

Computers, Inc. Mouse Pad Inventory			
Date	Units	$/Unit	Total
Beginning Inventory	1,000	$ 5.25	$ 5,250.00
Purchases:			
Jan. 3	300	5.30	1,590.00
June 20	150	5.60	840.00
Sept. 15	200	5.80	1,160.00
Nov. 29	150	5.90	885.00
Goods [illegible]			
[illegible]	[illegible]		[illegible]

Remember: FIFO ending inventory is calculated using the cost of the most recent purchases. Start with 11/29 and then add other purchases until you reach the number of units in ending inventory.

Irwin/McGraw-Hill

FIFO - Example

Date	Beg. Inv.	Purchases	End. Inv.	Cost of Goods Sold
Nov. 29		150@$5.90	150@$5.90	
Units			150	

Irwin/McGraw-Hill

FIFO - Example

Date	Beg. Inv.	Purchases	End. Inv.	Cost of Goods Sold
Sept. 15		200@$5.80	200@$5.80	
Nov. 29		150@$5.90	150@$5.90	
Units			350	

Irwin/McGraw-Hill

FIFO - Example

Date	Beg. Inv.	Purchases	End. Inv.	Cost of Goods Sold
June 20		150@$5.60	150@$5.60	
Sept. 15		200@$5.80	200@$5.80	
Nov. 29		150@$5.90	150@$5.90	
Units			500	

FIFO - Example

Date	Beg. Inv.	Purchases	End. Inv.	Cost of Goods Sold
Jan. 3		300@$5.30	300@$5.30	
June 20		150@$5.60	150@$5.60	
Sept. 15		200@$5.80	200@$5.80	
Nov. 29		150@$5.90	150@$5.90	
Units			800	

FIFO - Example

Date	Beg. Inv.	Purchases	End. Inv.	Cost of Goods Sold
	1,000@$5.2 →			600@$5.25
	→		400@$5.25	
Jan. 3		300@$5.30	300@$5.30	
June 20		150@$5.60	150@$5.60	
Sept. 15		200@$5.80	200@$5.80	
Nov. 29		150@$5.90	150@$5.90	
Units			1,200	600

Now, we have allocated the cost to all 1,200 units in ending inventory.

FIFO - Example

Date	Beg. Inv.	Purchases	End. Inv.	Cost of Goods Sold
	1,000@$5.2			600@$5.25
			400@$5.25	
Jan. 3		300@$5.30	300@$5.30	
June 20		150@$5.60	150@$5.60	
Sept. 15		200@$5.80	200@$5.80	
Nov. 29		150@$5.90	150@$5.90	
Units			1,200	600
Costs			$6,575	$3,150
Cost of Goods Available for Sale			$9,725	

Last-In, First-Out

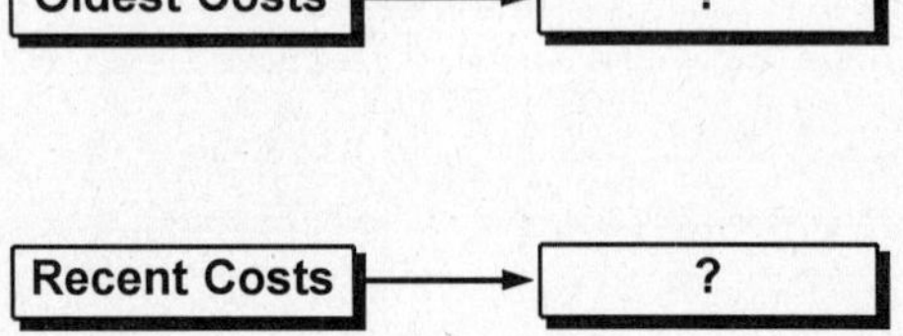

Last-In, First-Out

The schedule on the next screen shows the mouse pad inventory for Computers, Inc.

The physical inventory count shows 1,200 mouse pads in ending inventory.

Use the LIFO inventory method to determine:

(1) Ending inventory cost.

(2) Cost of goods sold.

LIFO - Example

Computers, Inc. Mouse Pad Inventory			
Date	Units	$/Unit	Total
Beginning Inventory	1,000	$ 5.25	$ 5,250.00
Purchases:			
Jan. 3	300	5.30	1,590.00
June 20	150	5.60	840.00
Sept. 15	200	5.80	1,160.00
Nov. 29	150	5.90	885.00
Goods Available for Sale	1,800		$ 9,725.00
Ending Inventory	1200		?
Cost of Goods Sold	600		?

LIFO - Example

Computers, Inc. Mouse Pad Inventory			
Date	Units	$/Unit	Total
Beginning Inventory	1,000	$ 5.25	$ 5,250.00
Purchases:			
Jan. 3	300	5.30	1,590.00
June 20	150	5.60	840.00
Sept. 15	200	5.80	1,160.00
Nov. 29	150	5.90	885.00
Goods Available			

Remember: LIFO ending inventory is calculated using the cost of the oldest purchases. Start with beginning inventory and then add other purchases until you reach the number of units in ending inventory.

LIFO - Example

Date	Beg. Inv.	Purchases	End. Inv.	Cost of Goods Sold
	1,000@$5.25 →		1,000@$5.25	
Units			1,000	

LIFO - Example

Date	Beg. Inv.	Purchases	End. Inv.	Cost of Goods Sold
	1,000@$5.25		1,000@$5.25	
Jan. 3		300@$5.30	200@$5.30	
Units			1,200	

Now, we have allocated the cost to all 1,200 units in ending inventory.

LIFO - Example

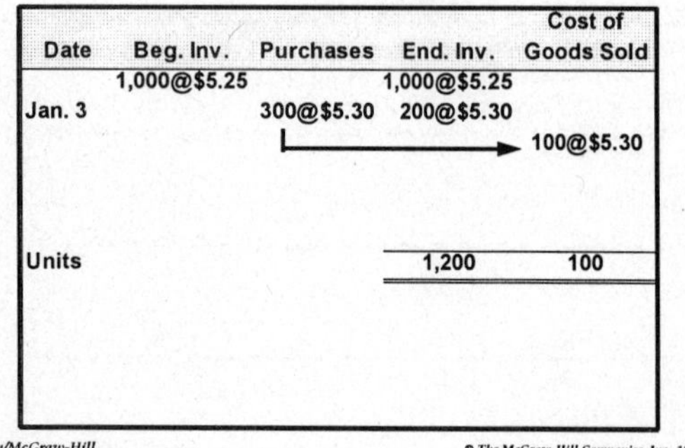

Date	Beg. Inv.	Purchases	End. Inv.	Cost of Goods Sold
	1,000@$5.25		1,000@$5.25	
Jan. 3		300@$5.30	200@$5.30	
				100@$5.30
Units			1,200	100

LIFO - Example

Date	Beg. Inv.	Purchases	End. Inv.	Cost of Goods Sold
	1,000@$5.25		1,000@$5.25	
Jan. 3		300@$5.30	200@$5.30	
				100@$5.30
June 20		150@$5.60		150@$5.60
Sept. 15		200@$5.80		200@$5.80
Nov. 29		150@$5.90		150@$5.90
Units			1,200	600
Costs			$6,310	$3,415
Cost of Goods Available for Sale			$9,725	

Weighted-Average

Weighted-average cost (WAC) per unit

$$\frac{\text{Beginning inventory cost} + \text{Current purchase cost}}{\text{Beginning inventory units} + \text{Current purchase units}}$$

Ending Inventory

Ending Inv. = Units in Ending Inv. × WAC per Unit

Cost of Good Sold

CGS = Units Sold × WAC per Unit

Weighted-Average - Example

The schedule on the next screen shows the mouse pad inventory for Computers, Inc.

The physical inventory count shows 1,200 mouse pads in ending inventory.

Use the weighted-average inventory method to determine:

(1) Ending inventory cost.

(2) Cost of goods sold.

Weighted-Average - Example

Computers, Inc.
Mouse Pad Inventory

Date	Units	$/Unit	Total
Beginning Inventory	1,000	$ 5.25	$ 5,250.00
Purchases:			
Jan. 3	300	5.30	1,590.00
June 20	150	5.60	840.00
Sept. 15	200	5.80	1,160.00
Nov. 29	150	5.90	885.00
Goods Available for Sale	1,800		$ 9,725.00
Ending Inventory	1200		?
Cost of Goods Sold	600		?

Weighted-Average - Example

Weighted-Average Cost per Unit:

Ending Inventory:

Cost of Goods Sold:

Specific Identification

- Specific cost of each inventory item is known.
- Used with small volume, high dollar inventory.

Comparison of Methods

Computers, Inc.
Income Statement
For Year Ended December 31, 1999

	Weighted Average	FIFO	LIFO
Net sales	$ 25,000	$ 25,000	$ 25,000
Cost of goods sold:			
Merchandise inventory, 12/31/98	$ 5,250	$ 5,250	$ 5,250
Net purchases	4,475	4,475	4,475
Goods available for sale	$ 9,725	$ 9,725	$ 9,725
Merchandise inventory, 12/31/99	6,483	6,575	6,310
Cost of goods sold	$ 3,242	$ 3,150	$ 3,415
Gross profit from sales	$ 21,758	$ 21,850	$ 21,585
Operating expenses:	750	750	750
Income before taxes	$ 21,008	$ 21,100	$ 20,835
Income taxes expense (30%)	6,302	6,330	6,251
Net income	$ 14,706	$ 14,770	$ 14,585

* Tax expense amounts were rounded.

Comparison of Methods

In periods of rising prices, FIFO results in the highest ending inventory, gross profit, tax expense, and net income, and the lowest cost of goods sold.

1999

		FIFO	LIFO
		$ 25,000	$ 25,000
		$ 5,250	$ 5,250
Net purchases	4,475	4,475	4,475
Goods available for sale	$ 9,725	$ 9,725	$ 9,725
Merchandise inventory, 12/31/99	6,483	6,575	6,310
Cost of goods sold	$ 3,242	$ 3,150	$ 3,415
Gross profit from sales	$ 21,758	$ 21,850	$ 21,585
Operating expenses:	750	750	750
Income before taxes	$ 21,008	$ 21,100	$ 20,835
Income taxes expense (30%)	6,302	6,330	6,251
Net income	$ 14,706	$ 14,770	$ 14,585

* Tax expense amounts were rounded.

Comparison of Methods

In periods of rising prices, LIFO results in the lowest ending inventory, gross profit, tax expense, and net income, and the highest cost of goods sold.

			LIFO
			$ 25,000
Merchandise inventory, 12/31/98	$ 5,250	$ 5,250	$ 5,250
Net purchases	4,475	4,475	4,475
Goods available for sale	$ 9,725	$ 9,725	$ 9,725
Merchandise inventory, 12/31/99	6,483	6,575	6,310
Cost of goods sold	$ 3,242	$ 3,150	$ 3,415
Gross profit from sales	$ 21,758	$ 21,850	$ 21,585
Operating expenses:	750	750	750
Income before taxes	$ 21,008	$ 21,100	$ 20,835
Income taxes expense (30%)	6,302	6,330	6,251
Net income	$ 14,706	$ 14,770	$ 14,585

* Tax expense amounts were rounded.

Comparison of Methods

As you might expect, the results of using the weighted-average method fall between FIFO and LIFO.

ters, Inc.
tatement
ecember 31, 1999

	Weighted Average	FIFO	LIFO
	$ 25,000	$ 25,000	$ 25,000
	$ 5,250	$ 5,250	$ 5,250
Net purchases	4,475	4,475	4,475
Goods available for sale	$ 9,725	$ 9,725	$ 9,725
Merchandise inventory, 12/31/99	6,483	6,575	6,310
Cost of goods sold	$ 3,242	$ 3,150	$ 3,415
Gross profit from sales	$ 21,758	$ 21,850	$ 21,585
Operating expenses:	750	750	750
Income before taxes	$ 21,008	$ 21,100	$ 20,835
Income taxes expense (30%)	6,302	6,330	6,251
Net income	$ 14,706	$ 14,770	$ 14,585

* Tax expense amounts were rounded.

Alternative Inventory Costing Methods in Practice

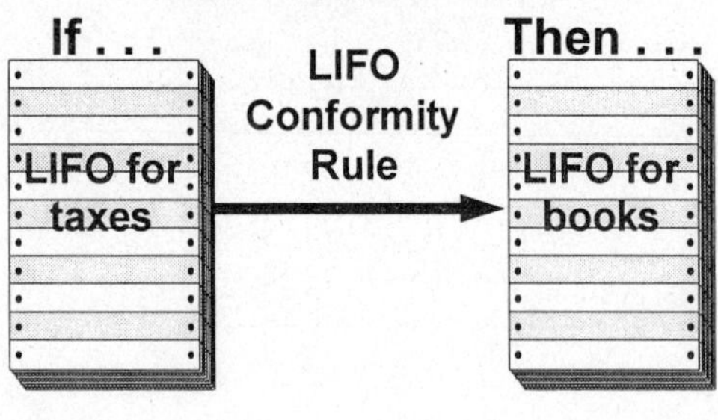

Alternative Inventory Costing Methods in Practice

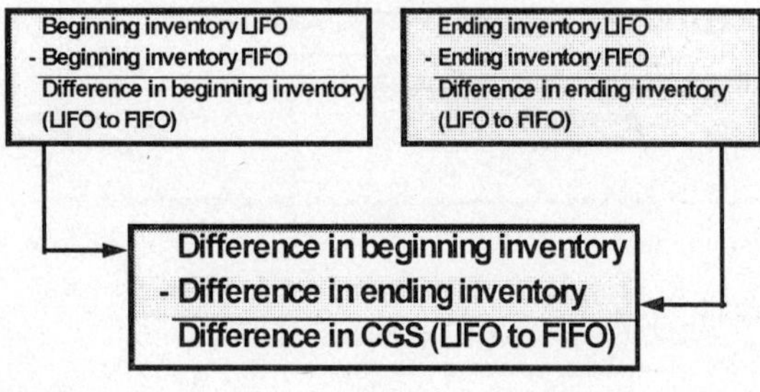

LIFO and Financial Statement Analysis

- **Inventory Turnover**

$$\text{Inventory Turnover} = \frac{\text{Cost of Goods Sold}}{\text{Average Inventory}}$$

Average Inventory is calculated as:

(Beginning Inventory + Ending Inventory) ÷ 2

This ratio is often used to measure the liquidity (nearness to cash) of the inventory.

Lower of Cost or Market

- **Ending inventory is reported at the lower of cost or market (LCM).**
- **Market is either:**
  - ❖**Replacement cost** - the current purchase price of identical goods.
  - ❖**Net realizable value** - the expected sales price less selling costs.

Lower of Cost or Market

When the market cost of the inventory is less than the historical cost, the loss is immediately recorded.

GENERAL JOURNAL — Page 34

Date		Description	Post. Ref.	Debit	Credit
		Cost of Goods Sold		XXX	
		Inventory			XXX

Focus on Cash Flows

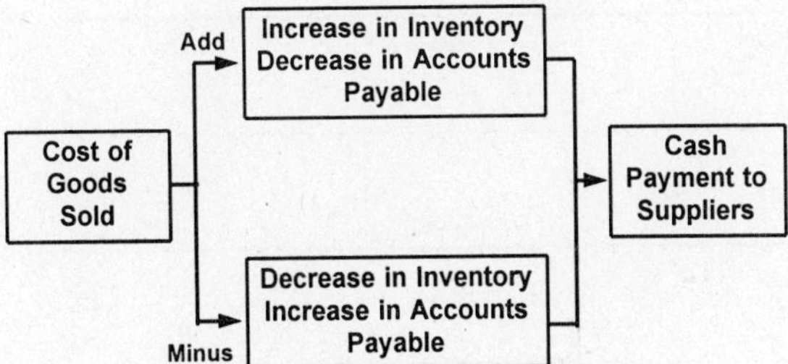

Comparison of Periodic and Perpetual Systems

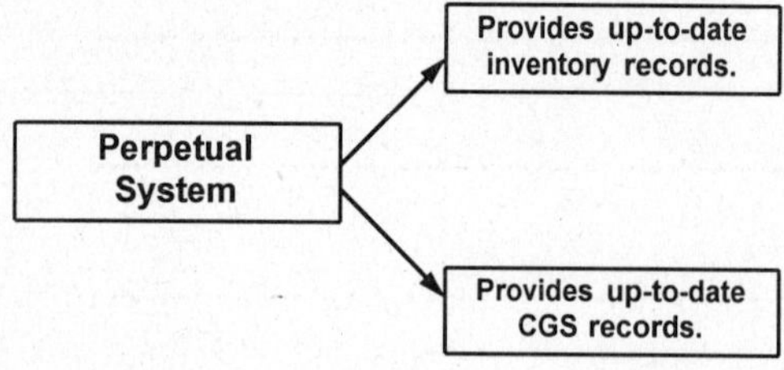

Perpetual System
Provides up-to-date inventory records.
Provides up-to-date CGS records.

Comparison of Periodic and Perpetual Systems

Model	Source of Information	
	Periodic System	Perpetual System
Beginning Inventory	Carried over from prior period	Carried over from prior period
Add: Purchases	Accumulated in the Purchases account	Accumulated in the Inventory account
Less: Ending Inventory	Measured at end of period by physical inventory count	Perpetual record updated at every sale
Cost of Goods Sold	Computed as a residual amount at end of period	Measured at every sale based on perpetual record

Now, let's compare the various entries that are made when using the periodic and perpetual inventory systems.

Comparison of Periodic and Perpetual Systems

Transaction	Periodic	Perpetual
Merchandise purchased from supplier on account.	Purchases XX Accounts Payable XX	Inventory XX Accounts Payable XX

Comparison of Periodic and Perpetual Systems

Transaction	Periodic	Perpetual
Merchandise purchased from supplier on account.	Purchases XX Accounts Payable XX	Inventory XX Accounts Payable XX
Merchandise returned to supplier.	Accounts Payable XX Purchases Returns & Allow. XX	Accounts Payable XX Inventory XX

Purchases Returns and Allowances is subtracted from Purchases on the income statement.

Comparison of Periodic and Perpetual Systems

Transaction	Periodic	Perpetual
Merchandise purchased from supplier on account.	Purchases XX Accounts Payable XX	Inventory XX Accounts Payable XX
Merchandise returned to supplier.	Accounts Payable XX Purchases Returns & Allow. XX	This entry is recorded at retail. X XX
Merchandise sold to customer on account.	Accounts Receivable XX Sales XX	Accounts Receivable XX Sales XX Cost of Goods Sold XX Inventory XX

This entry is recorded at cost.

Comparison of Periodic and Perpetual Systems

Transaction	Periodic			Perpetual		
Merchandise returned by customer.	Sales Returns and Allow.	XX		Sales Returns and Allow.	XX	
	Accounts Receivable		XX	Accounts Receivable		XX
				Inventory	XX	
				Cost of Goods Sold		XX

This is recorded at retail.

This entry is recorded at cost.

Irwin/McGraw-Hill

Comparison of Periodic and Perpetual Systems

Transaction	Periodic			Perpetual		
Merchandise returned by customer.	Sales Returns and Allow.	XX		Sales Returns and Allow.	XX	
	Accounts Receivable		XX	Accounts Receivable		XX
				Inventory	XX	
				Cost of Goods Sold		XX
At end of accounting period.	Cost of Goods Sold	XX		No entry.		
	Inventory (beginning)		XX			
	Purchases		XX			
	Inventory (ending)	XX				
	Cost of Goods Sold		XX			

Irwin/McGraw-Hill

Cash Discounts

I can offer you a 2 percent sales discount if you buy from me.
He's offering me a 2 percent purchase discount if I buy from him.

Irwin/McGraw-Hill

Purchases Discounts

On July 6, Office City sold $550 of merchandise to Kelly's Flowers on credit. The credit terms are 2/10, n/30. Kelly's Flowers pays for the merchandise on July 14.

Prepare the entry to record the cash payment on Kelly's Flowers' records.

Purchases Discounts

$550 × 2% = $11 Purchases Discount

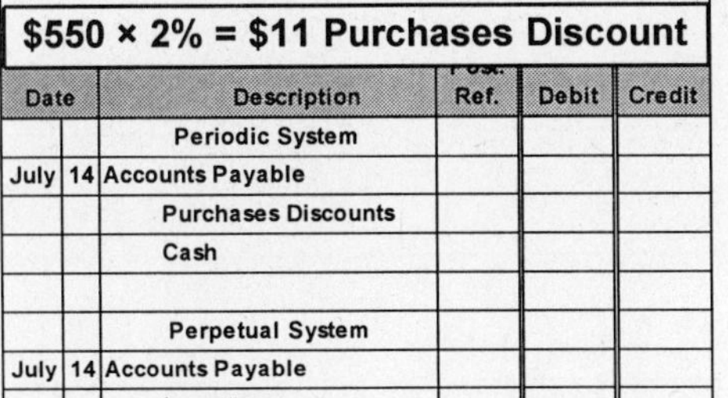

Date		Description	Post. Ref.	Debit	Credit
		Periodic System			
July	14	Accounts Payable			
		Purchases Discounts			
		Cash			
		Perpetual System			
July	14	Accounts Payable			
		Inventory			
		Cash			

Purchases Discounts

If Kelly's Flowers paid outside of the discount period, the full purchase price would be due and a purchase discount would not be recorded.

GENERAL JOURNAL Page 25

Date		Description	Post. Ref.	Debit	Credit
		Accounts Payable			
		Cash			

The End of Chapter 7

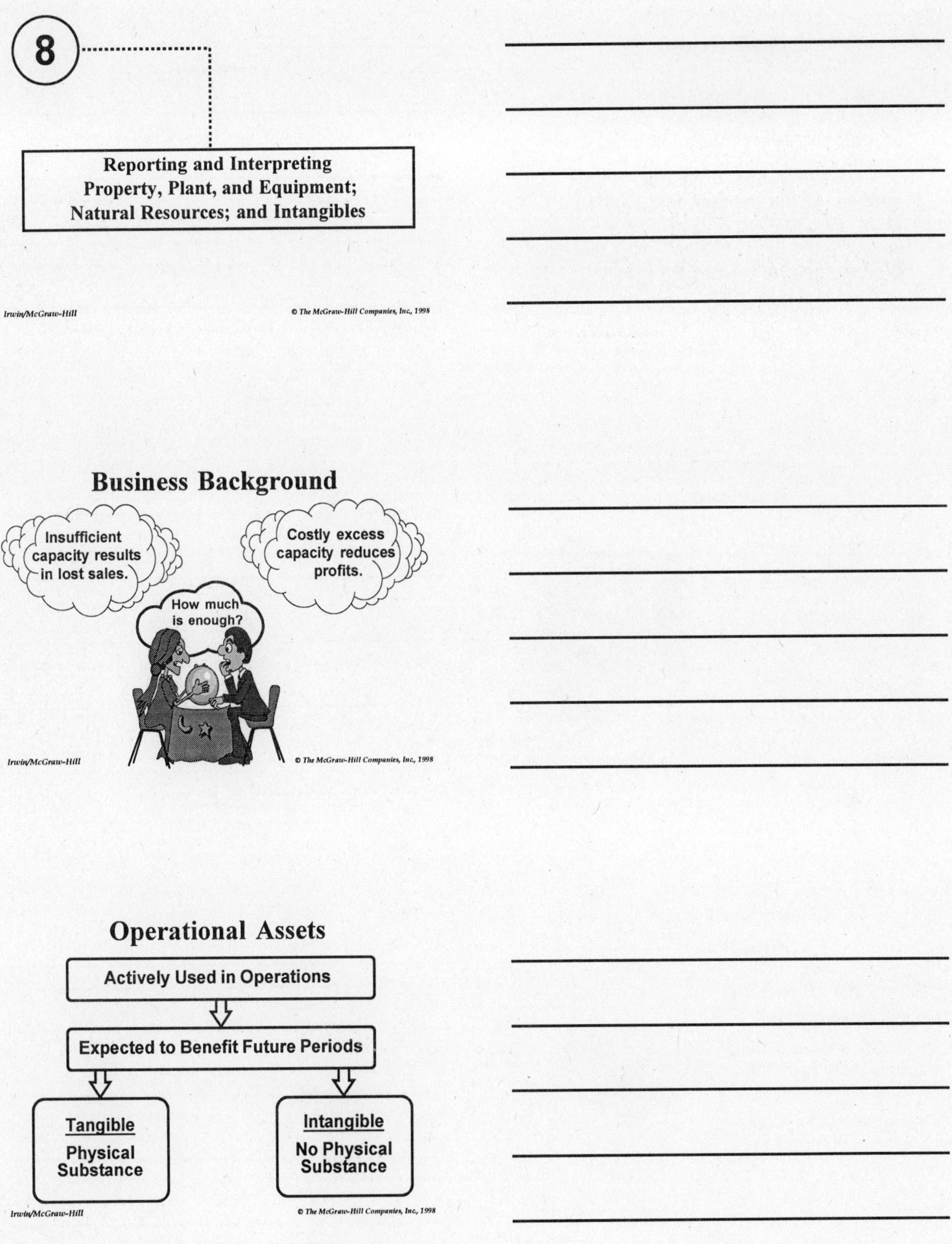
8
Reporting and Interpreting
Property, Plant, and Equipment;
Natural Resources; and Intangibles
Irwin/McGraw-Hill
© The McGraw-Hill Companies, Inc, 1998
Business Background
Insufficient capacity results in lost sales.
Costly excess capacity reduces profits.
How much is enough?
Irwin/McGraw-Hill
© The McGraw-Hill Companies, Inc, 1998
Operational Assets
Actively Used in Operations
Expected to Benefit Future Periods
Tangible
Physical Substance
Intangible
No Physical Substance
Irwin/McGraw-Hill
© The McGraw-Hill Companies, Inc, 1998

Acquisition Cost
General Rule

Acquisition cost includes the purchase price and all expenditures needed to prepare the asset for its intended use.

Acquisition cost does not include financing charges and cash discounts.

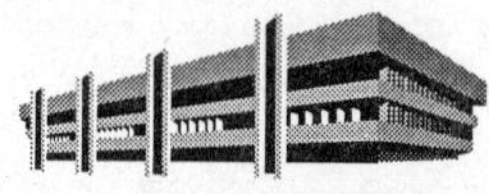

Irwin/McGraw-Hill

Acquisition Cost
Buildings

- Purchase price
- Architectural fees
- Cost of permits
- Excavation costs
- Construction costs

Irwin/McGraw-Hill

© The McGraw-Hill Companies, Inc, 1998

Acquisition Cost
Equipment

- Purchase price
- Installation costs
- Modification to building necessary to install equipment
- Transportation costs

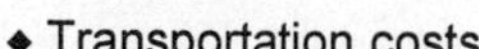

Irwin/McGraw-Hill

© The McGraw-Hill Companies, Inc, 1998

Acquisition Cost
Land

- Purchase price
- Real estate commissions
- Title insurance premiums
- Delinquent taxes
- Surveying fees
- Title search and transfer fees

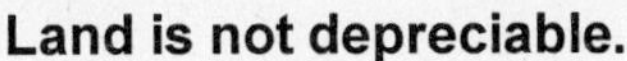

Land is not depreciable.

Acquisition for Cash

On June 1, equipment was purchased for $10,000 cash.

GENERAL JOURNAL					Page 8
Date		Description	Post. Ref.	Debit	Credit

Acquisition for Debt

On May 14, equipment was purchased for $10,000 cash and a $40,000 note payable.

GENERAL JOURNAL					Page 8
Date		Description	Post. Ref.	Debit	Credit

Acquisition for Noncash Consideration

Record at the current market value of the consideration given, or the current market value of the asset acquired, whichever is more clearly evident.

Acquisition for Noncash Consideration

On July 7, equipment was acquired in exchange for 1,000 shares of $1 par stock with a market value of $15 per share.

GENERAL JOURNAL					Page 8
Date		Description	Post. Ref.	Debit	Credit

Acquisition by Construction

Asset cost includes:

- All materials and labor traceable to the construction.
- A reasonable amount of overhead.
- Interest on debt incurred during the construction.

Acquisition as a Basket Purchase

The total cost of a combined purchase of land and building is separated on the basis of their relative market values.

Acquisition as a Basket Purchase Example

On January 1, UpCo purchased land and building for $200,000 cash. The appraised values are building, $162,500, and land, $87,500. How much of the $200,000 purchase price will be charged to the building and land accounts?

Continue 

Acquisition as a Basket Purchase Example

Asset	Appraised Value	% of Value	Purchase Price	Assigned Cost
	a	b*	c	b × c
Land	$ 87,500	35%		
Building	162,500	65%		
Total	$ 250,000	100%		

* $87,500 ÷ $250,000 = 35%

Repairs, Maintenance, and Additions

Type of Expenditure	Capital or Revenue	Identifying Characteristics
Ordinary repairs and maintenance	Revenue	1. Maintains normal operating condition 2. Does not increase productivity 3. Does not extend life beyond original estimate
Extraordinary repairs	Capital	1. Major overhauls or partial replacements 2. Extends life beyond original estimate
Additions	Capital	1. Increases productivity 2. May extend useful life 3. Improvements or expansions

Irwin/McGraw-Hill

Capital and Revenue Expenditures

To Capitalize or to Expense?

	Financial Statement Effect			
Treatment	Statement	Expense	Current Income	Current Taxes
Capital Expenditure	Balance sheet account debited	Deferred	Higher	Higher
Revenue Expenditure	Income statement account debited	Currently recognized	Lower	Lower

Many companies have policies expensing all expenditures below a certain amount according to the materiality constraint.

Irwin/McGraw-Hill

Depreciation

Depreciation is a cost allocation process that systematically and rationally matches acquisition costs of operational assets with periods benefited by their use.

Balance Sheet

Acquisition Cost

(Unused)

Cost Allocation →

Income Statement

Expense

(Used)

Irwin/McGraw-Hill

Depreciation

Depreciation Expense → Depreciation for the current year → Income Statement

Accumulated Depreciation → Total of depreciation to date on an asset → Balance Sheet

Depreciation on the Balance Sheet

Property, plant, and equipment:	
Land and buildings	$150,000
Machinery and equipment	200,000
Office furniture and equipment	175,000
Land improvements	50,000
Total	$575,000
Less Accumulated depreciation	(122,000)
Net property, plant, and equipment	$453,000

Net property, plant, and equipment is the undepreciated cost (book value) of the plant assets.

Book value ≠ market value

Depreciation Concepts

The calculation of depreciation requires three amounts for each asset:

❶ Acquisition cost.

❷ Estimated useful life.

❸ Estimated residual value.

Alternative Depreciation Methods

❶ Straight-line

❷ Units-of-production

❸ Accelerated Method: declining balance

Straight-Line Method

Example

$$\text{Depreciation Expense per Year} = \frac{\text{Cost} - \text{Residual Value}}{\text{Life in Years}}$$

On January 1, 1995, equipment was purchased for $50,000 cash. The equipment has an estimated useful life of 5 years and an estimated residual value of $5,000.

Straight-Line Method

Example

Year	Depreciation Expense (debit)	Accumulated Depreciation (credit)	Accumulated Depreciation Balance	Undepreciated Balance (book value)
				$ 50,000
1995	$ 9,000	$ 9,000	$ 9,000	41,000
1996	9,000	9,000	18,000	32,000
1997	9,000	9,000	27,000	23,000
1998	9,000	9,000	36,000	14,000
1999	9,000	9,000	45,000	5,000
	$ 36,000	$ 36,000		

Residual Value

Units-of-Production Method

Step 1:

$$\text{Depreciation Rate} = \frac{\text{Cost - Residual Value}}{\text{Life in Units of Production}}$$

Step 2:

$$\text{Depreciation Expense} = \text{Depreciation Rate} \times \text{Number of Units Produced for the Year}$$

Units-of-Production Method
Example

On January 1, 1995, equipment was purchased for $50,000 cash. The equipment is expected to produce 100,000 units during its useful life and has an estimated residual value of $5,000.

If 22,000 units were produced in 1995, what is the amount of depreciation expense?

Units-of-Production Method
Example

Step 1:

$$\text{Depreciation Rate} = \frac{\$50{,}000 - \$5{,}000}{100{,}000 \text{ units}} = \$.45 \text{ per unit}$$

Units-of-Production Method
Example

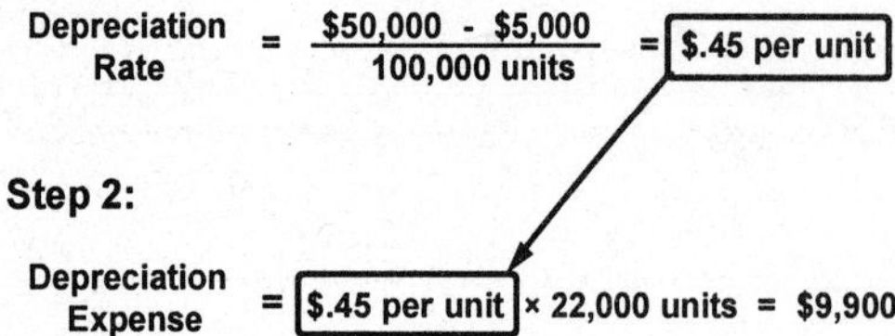

Step 1:
Depreciation Rate = $50,000 - $5,000 / 100,000 units = $.45 per unit
Step 2:
Depreciation Expense = $.45 per unit × 22,000 units = $9,900

Irwin/McGraw-Hill

Units-of-Production Method
Example

Year	Units	Depreciation Expense	Accumulated Depreciation Balance	Undepreciated Balance (book value)
				$ 50,000
1995	22,000	$ 9,900	$ 9,900	40,100
1996	28,000	12,600	22,500	27,500
1997	-	-	22,500	27,500
1998	32,000	14,400	36,900	13,100
1999	18,000	8,100	45,000	5,000
	100,000	$ 45,000		

Residual Value

No depreciation expense if the equipment is idle.

Irwin/McGraw-Hill

Accelerated Depreciation

Accelerated depreciation matches higher depreciation expense with higher revenues in the early years of an asset's useful life when the asset is more efficient.

	Depreciation Expense	Repair Expense
Early Years	High	Low
Later Years	Low	High

Irwin/McGraw-Hill

Double-Declining-Balance Method

Declining balance rate of 2 is double-declining-balance (DDB) rate.

$$\text{Annual Depreciation expense} = \text{Book Value} \times \left(\frac{2}{\text{Useful Life in Years}}\right)$$

Book Value: Cost – Accumulated Depreciation

Annual computation ignores residual value.

Double-Declining-Balance Method
Example

On January 1, 1995, equipment was purchased for $50,000 cash. The equipment has an estimated useful life of 5 years and an estimated residual value of $5,000.

Calculate the depreciation expense for 1995 and 1996.

Double-Declining-Balance Method
Example

$$\text{Annual Depreciation expense} = \text{Book Value} \times \left(\frac{2}{\text{Useful Life in Years}}\right)$$

1995 Depreciation:

$$\$50{,}000 \times \left(\frac{2}{5\text{ years}}\right) = \boxed{\$20{,}000}$$

1996 Depreciation:

$$(\$50{,}000 - \boxed{\$20{,}000}) \times \left(\frac{2}{5\text{ years}}\right) = \$12{,}000$$

Double-Declining-Balance Method
Example

Year	Depreciation Expense (debit)	Accumulated Depreciation Balance	Undepreciated Balance (book value)
			$ 50,000
1995	$ 20,000	$ 20,000	30,000
1996	12,000	32,000	18,000
1997	7,200	39,200	10,800
1998	4,320	43,520	6,480
1999	1,480	45,000	5,000
	$ 45,000		

We usually have to force depreciation expense in the latter years to an amount that brings BV to residual value.

Comparison of Methods:
Straight-Line Method

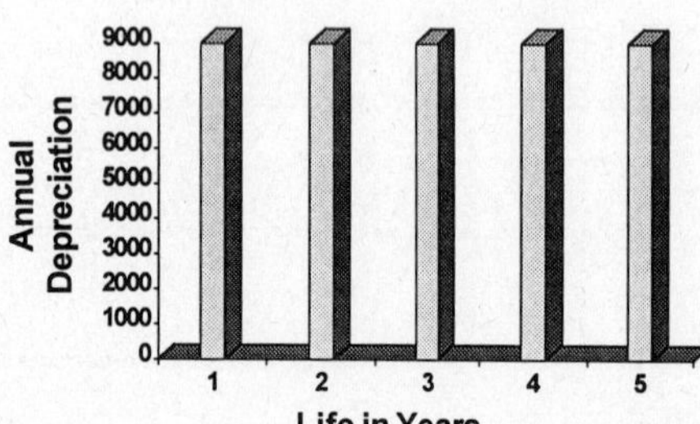

Comparison of Methods:
Units-of-Production Method

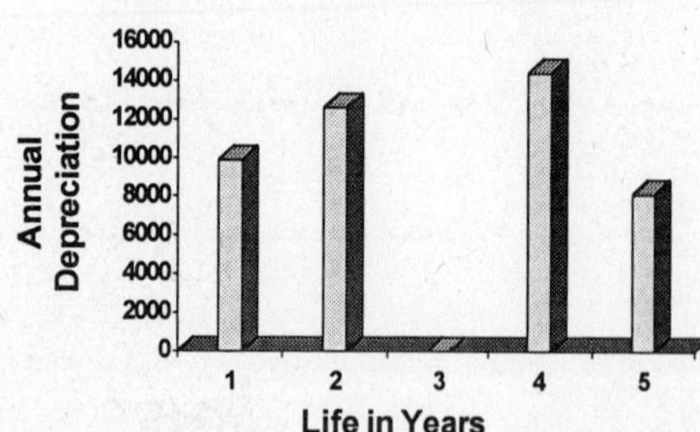

Comparison of Methods: Double-Declining-Balance Method

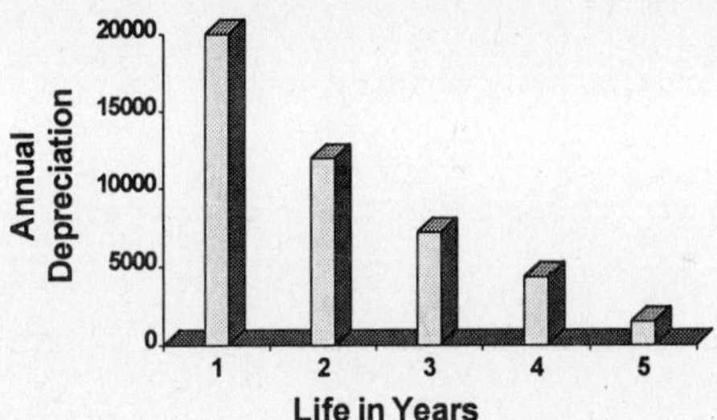

Comparison of Methods

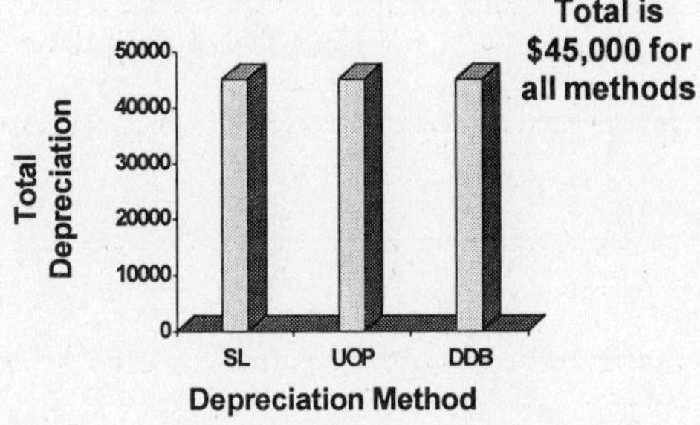

Comparison of Methods

More than 95 percent of companies use the straight-line method for financial reports.

Other methods may be used for tax purposes.

Depreciation and Federal Income Tax

Most corporations use the Modified Accelerated Cost Recovery System (MACRS) for tax purposes.

MACRS depreciation provides for rapid write-off of an asset's cost in order to stimulate new investment.

Depreciation Methods in Other Countries

- In addition to the methods already discussed, other methods are commonly used in other countries.
- Several countries, including Australia, Brazil, England, and Mexico, allow depreciation based on the current fair value of an asset.

Changes in Depreciation Estimates

Estimated residual value → So depreciation is an estimate. ← Estimated useful life

Over the life of an asset, new information may come to light that indicates the original estimates were inaccurate.

Changes in Depreciation Estimates

If our estimates change, depreciation is:

$$\frac{\text{Book value at date of change} - \text{Residual value at date of change}}{\text{Remaining useful life at date of change}}$$

Changes in Depreciation Estimates
Example

On January 1, 1996, equipment was purchased that cost $30,000, has a useful life of 10 years and no salvage value. During 1999, the useful life was revised to 8 years total (5 years remaining).

Calculate depreciation expense for the year ended December 31, 1999, using the straight-line method.

Changes in Depreciation Estimates
Example

Asset cost	$ 30,000
Accumulated depreciation, 12/31/98	
($3,000 per year × 3 years)	9,000
Remaining book value	21,000
Divide by remaining life	÷ 5
Revised annual depreciation	$ 4,200

Effect on Statement of Cash Flows

- Depreciation expense, unlike most other expenses, does not require a cash outflow.
- Because depreciation is tax deductible, it reduces the cash outflow related to taxes.

Disposal of Operational Assets

- **Voluntary disposals:**
  - ❖Sale
  - ❖Trade-in
  - ❖Retirement
- **Involuntary disposals:**
  - ❖Fire
  - ❖Accident

Disposal of Operational Assets

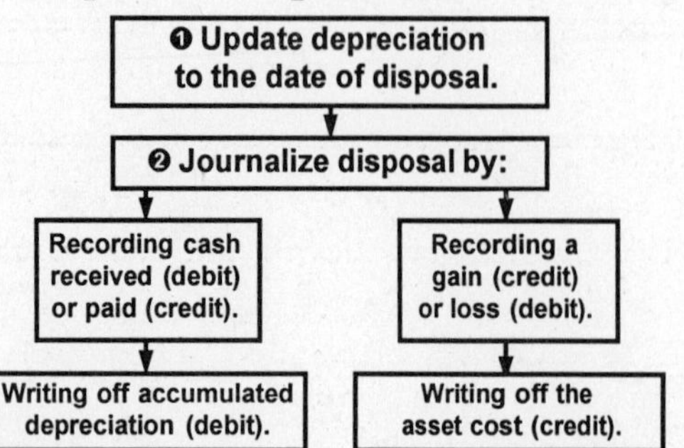
➊ Update depreciation to the date of disposal.
➋ Journalize disposal by:
Recording cash received (debit) or paid (credit).
Recording a gain (credit) or loss (debit).
Writing off accumulated depreciation (debit).
Writing off the asset cost (credit).

Disposal of Operational Assets

If Cash > BV, record a gain (credit).
If Cash < BV, record a loss (debit).
If Cash = BV, no gain or loss.

FOR SALE

Disposal of Operational Assets
Example

On September 30, 1999, Evans Company sold a machine that originally cost $100,000 for $60,000 cash. The machine was placed in service on January 1, 1994. It was depreciated using the straight-line method with an estimated salvage value of $20,000 and a useful life of 10 years.

Disposal of Operational Assets
Question

The amount of depreciation recorded on September 30, 1999 to bring depreciation up to date is:

a. $8,000.
b. $6,000.
c. $4,000.
d. $2,000.

Disposal of Operational Assets
Question

After updating the depreciation, the machine's book value on September 30, 1999 is:

a. $54,000.
b. $46,000.
c. $40,000.
d. $60,000.

Disposal of Operational Assets
Question

The machine's sale resulted in:

a. a gain of $6,000.
b. a gain of $4,000.
c. a loss of $6,000.
d. a loss of $4,000.

Disposal of Operational Assets
Example

Prepare the journal entry to record Evans' sale of the machine on September 30, 1999.

GENERAL JOURNAL — Page 8

Date		Description	Post. Ref.	Debit	Credit

Natural Resources

Extracted from the natural environment.

A noncurrent asset presented at cost less accumulated depletion.

Examples: oil, coal, gold

Natural Resources

Total cost of asset is the cost of acquisition, exploration, and development.

Total cost is allocated over periods benefited by means of depletion.

Depletion is like depreciation.

Depletion of Natural Resources

Depletion is calculated using the units-of-production method.

Unit depletion rate is calculated as follows:

$$\frac{\text{Acquisition and Development Cost} - \text{Residual Value}}{\text{Estimated Recoverable Units}}$$

Depletion of Natural Resources

Total depletion cost for a period is:

UNIT DEPLETION RATE × NUMBER OF UNITS EXTRACTED IN PERIOD

Total depletion cost → Inventory for sale → Cost of goods sold / Unsold Inventory

Natural Resources
Example

ABC Mining acquired a tract of land containing ore deposits. Total costs of acquisition and development were $1,000,000 and ABC estimated the land contained 40,000 tons of ore.

Natural Resources
Question

What is ABC's depletion rate?

a. **$40 per ton**
b. **$50 per ton**
c. **$25 per ton**
d. **$20 per ton**

Natural Resources
Question

For the year ABC mined and sold 13,000 tons. What is the total depletion cost for the year?

a. $300,000
b. $325,000
c. $225,000
d. $275,000

Natural Resources

Specialized plant assets may be required to extract the natural resource.

These assets are recorded in a separate account and depreciated.

Intangible Assets

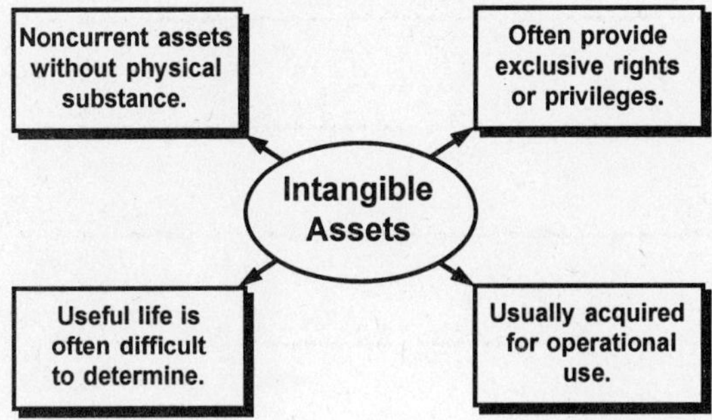
Noncurrent assets without physical substance.
Often provide exclusive rights or privileges.
Intangible Assets
Useful life is often difficult to determine.
Usually acquired for operational use.

Intangible Assets

Record at current cash equivalent cost, including purchase price, legal fees, and filing fees.

- Goodwill
- Patents
- Trademarks
- Copyrights
- Franchises
- Leaseholds

Intangible Assets

- Amortize over shorter of economic life or legal life, subject to a maximum of 40 years.
- Use straight-line method.
- Research and development costs are normally expensed as incurred.

Irwin/McGraw-Hill

© The McGraw-Hill Companies, Inc, 1998

Intangible Assets

Goodwill

Goodwill

- Occurs when one company buys another company.
- Only purchased goodwill is an intangible asset.
- The amount by which the purchase price exceeds the fair market value of net assets acquired.

Irwin/McGraw-Hill

© The McGraw-Hill Companies, Inc, 1998

Intangible Assets
Goodwill Example

Eddy Company paid $1,000,000 to purchase all of James Company's assets and assumed liabilities of $200,000. The acquired assets were appraised at a fair value of $900,000.

Intangible Assets
Goodwill Question

What amount of goodwill should be recorded on Eddy Company books?

a. $100,000
b. $200,000
c. $300,000
d. $400,000

Intangible Assets
Patents

Exclusive right granted by federal government to sell or manufacture an invention.

Cost is purchase price plus legal cost to defend.

Amortize cost over the shorter of useful life or 17 years.

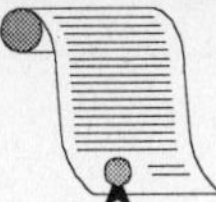

Intangible Assets
Trademarks

A symbol, design, or logo associated with a business.

VISA

Internally developed trademarks have no recorded asset cost.

Purchased trademarks are recorded at cost, and amortized over shorter of legal or economic life, or 40 years.

Intangible Assets
Copyrights

Exclusive right granted by the federal government to protect artistic or intellectual properties.

Legal life is life of creator plus 50 years.

Amortize cost over a period not to exceed 40 years.

Intangible Assets
Franchises

Legally protected right to sell products or provide services purchased by franchisee from franchisor.

Purchase price is intangible asset which is amortized over the shorter of the protected right or 40 years.

Intangible Assets
Leaseholds

- A lease is a contract to use property granted by lessor to lessee and rights granted under the lease are called a leasehold.
- A leasehold is recorded only if advance payment is involved. Otherwise periodic payments are rent expense.

Intangible Assets
Leasehold Improvements

Long-lived alterations made by lessee to leased property.

Leasehold improvements are recorded at cost and amortized over their useful life.

Asset Impairment

Impairment is the loss of a significant portion of the utility of an asset through . . .

- ❖Casualty.
- ❖Obsolescence.
- ❖Lack of demand for the asset's services.

A loss should be recognized when an asset suffers a permanent impairment.

This computer is
about to become
fully depreciated!

End of
Chapter 8

Irwin/McGraw-Hill

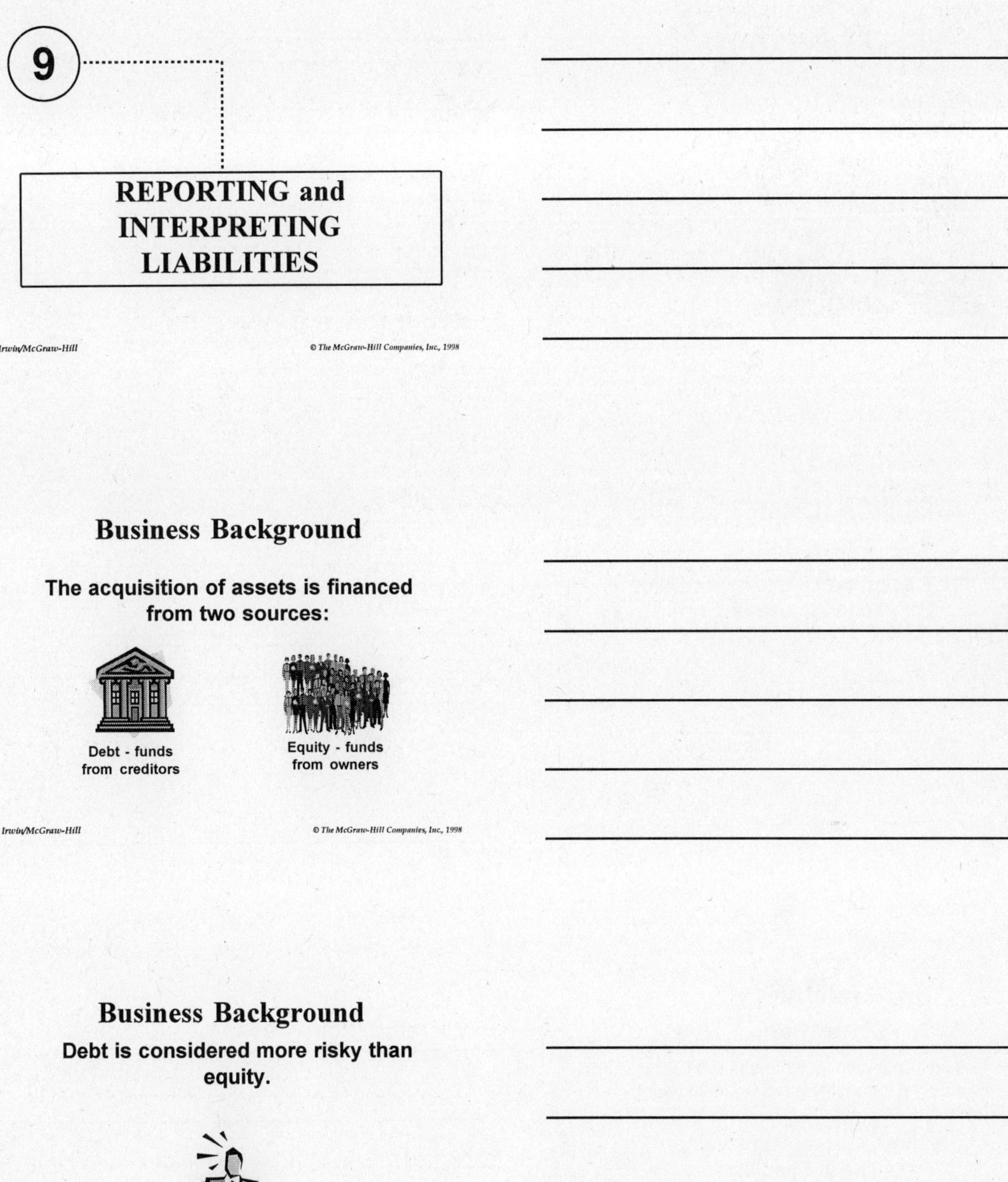

9
REPORTING and INTERPRETING LIABILITIES
Irwin/McGraw-Hill
© The McGraw-Hill Companies, Inc., 1998
Business Background
The acquisition of assets is financed from two sources:
Debt - funds from creditors
Equity - funds from owners
Irwin/McGraw-Hill
© The McGraw-Hill Companies, Inc., 1998

Business Background

Debt is considered more risky than equity.

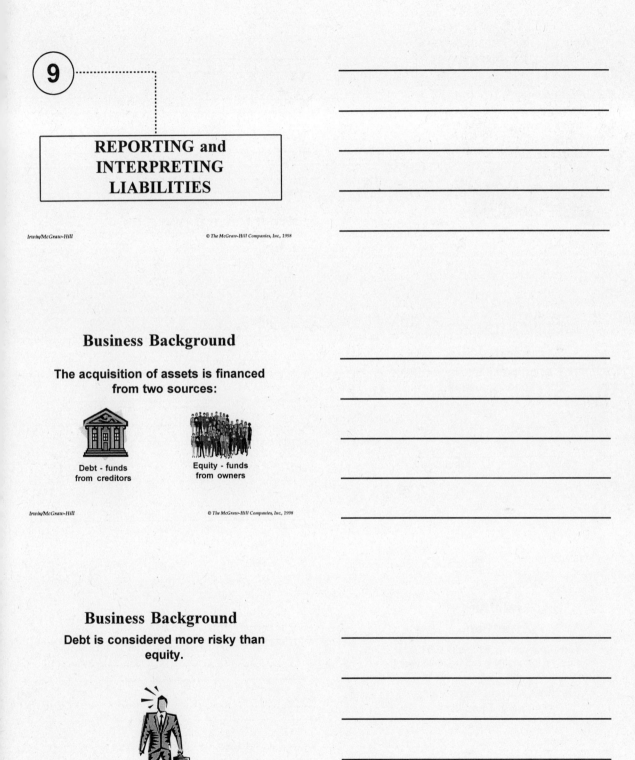

Business Background

Financial Leverage - Borrowing at one rate and investing at a higher rate.

Irwin/McGraw-Hill

Liabilities Defined and Classified

I.O.U.

Defined as probable future sacrifices of economic benefits.

Maturity = 1 year or less | Maturity > 1 year

_______ Liabilities | _______ Liabilities

Irwin/McGraw-Hill

Liabilities Question

Devon Mfg. borrows $100,000 from First Bank. The loan will be repaid in 20 years and has an annual interest rate of 8%.

Is this a current liability or a noncurrent liability?

Irwin/McGraw-Hill

Liabilities Question

Devon Mfg. borrows $100,000 from First Bank. The loan will be repaid in 20 years and has an annual interest rate of 8%.

How much will the liability be recorded for on Devon's books?

Evaluating Liquidity

An important indicator of a company's ability to meet its current obligations.

Two commonly used measures:

Current Ratio = Current Assets ÷ Current Liabilities

Working Capital = Current Assets - Current Liabilities

Liabilities Question

Devon Mfg. has current liabilities of $230,000 and current assets of $322,000.

What is Devon's current ratio?

Current Liabilities

Account Name	Also Called	Definition
Accounts Payable	Trade Accounts Payable	Obligations to pay for goods and services used in the basic operating activities of the business.
Accrued Liabilities	Accrued Expenses	Obligations related to expenses that have been incurred, but will not be paid until the subsequent period.
Deferred Revenues	Unearned Revenues	Obligations arising when cash is received prior to the related revenue being earned.
Note Payable	N/A	Portions of debt that are due within the next year or operating cycle.

Irwin/McGraw-Hill

Deferred Revenues and Service Obligations

Cash is collected from the customer before the revenue is actually earned.

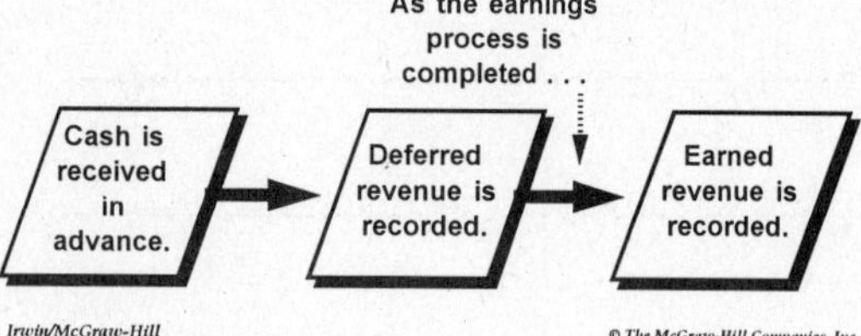

Irwin/McGraw-Hill

Deferred Revenues and Service Obligations - Example

On May 31, BIG CAR Magazine receives $120 for a 12-month subscription. Year-end is December 31.

How much revenue is recognized on December 31?

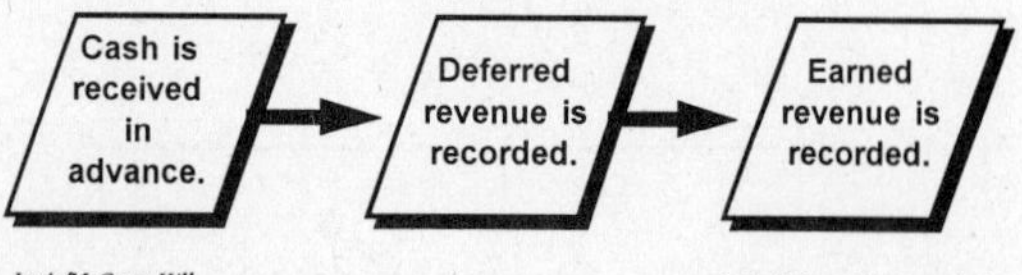

Cash is received in advance.
Deferred revenue is recorded.
Earned revenue is recorded.

Irwin/McGraw-Hill

Current Portion of Long-Term Payable

Any portion of a note payable that is due within one year, or one operating cycle, whichever is longer.

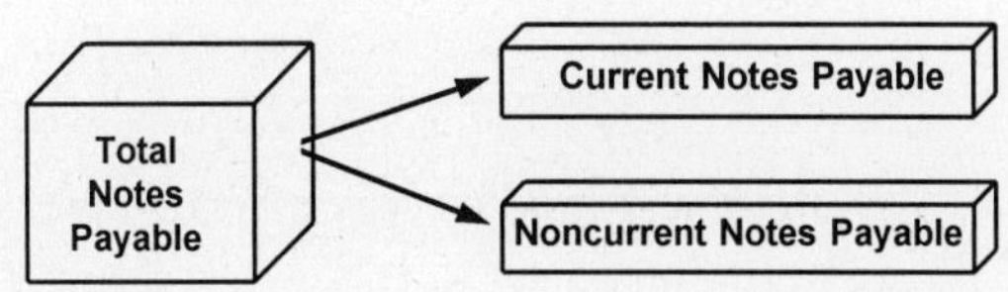

Interest Payable

The interest formula includes three variables that must be considered when computing interest:

Interest = Principal × Interest Rate × Time

Interest Payable

Cyber Corp. borrows $300,000 for 6 months at an annual interest rate of 9%. Compute the interest on the note for the loan period.

Long-Term Liabilities

Creditors often require the borrower to pledge specific assets as security for the long-term liability.

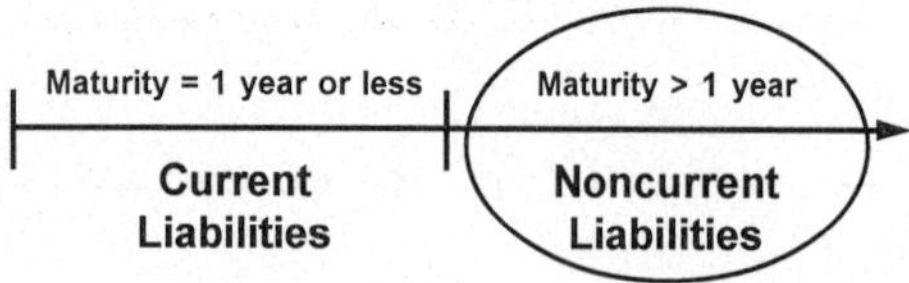

Sources for Long-Term Loans

Relatively small debt needs can be filled from single sources.

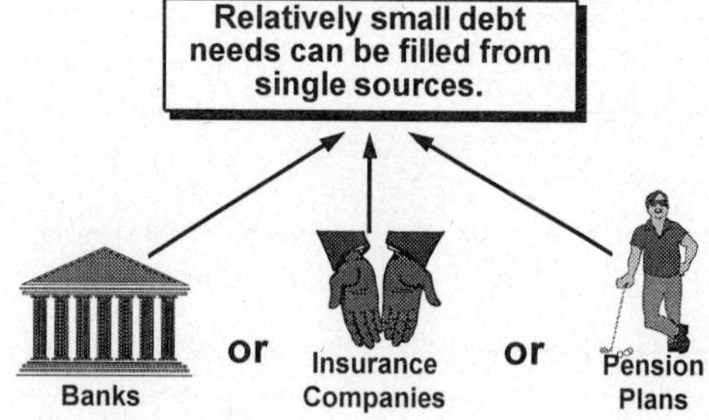

Sources for Publicly Issued Debt

Large debt needs are often filled by issuing bonds.

Borrowing in Foreign Currencies

- **When a company has operations in a foreign country, it often borrows in the local currency.**
  - ❖Reduces ____________________ **risk**.
  - ❖Because interest rates vary from country to country, companies may borrow in the foreign market with the lowest interest rate.

Borrowing in Foreign Currencies

- **Exchange rates are published daily in the Wall Street Journal.**
- **Eurodollars are U.S. dollars that are deposited in the European banking system.**
- **The European Currency Unit is an index of 10 European currencies that is used for borrowing.**

Deferred Taxes

GAAP is the set of rules for preparing financial statements.

Results in . . .

Financial statement income tax expense.

Usually. . .

The Internal Revenue Code is the set of rules for preparing tax returns.

Results in . . .

IRS income taxes payable.

Deferred Taxes - Example

Examine the December 31, 1998 information for X-Off Inc.

Revenues	$1,000,000
Depreciation Expense:	
Straight-line	200,000
Accelerated	320,000
Other Expenses	650,000

X-Off uses straight-line depreciation for financial reporting and accelerated depreciation for income tax reporting. X-Off's tax rate is 30%.

Irwin/McGraw-Hill

Deferred Taxes - Example

Compute X-Off's income tax expense and income tax payable.

	Income Statement	Tax Return	Difference
Revenues			
Less:			
Depreciation			
Other expenses			
Income before taxes			
× Tax rate			
Income taxes			

Irwin/McGraw-Hill

Accrued Retirement Benefits

- **Two basic types of employer provided retirement plans.**
  - ❖Defined contribution plans.
  - ❖Defined benefit plans.

Transfer of contributions

Pension payments

Employer

Retirement Plan Trustee

Retirees

Irwin/McGraw-Hill

Accrued Retirement Benefits: Defined Contribution Plans

- Regular, defined payments to the fund.
- The fund balance changes in value with the accumulation of ________________ and ________________.
- The employee's retirement benefit is based on the fund balance available at retirement.

Irwin/McGraw-Hill

Accrued Retirement Benefits: Defined Benefit Plans

- Retirement ____________ are defined by the company retirement plan.
- Contributions to the plan must be made so as to insure the availability of funds to pay the defined benefits.

Irwin/McGraw-Hill

Contingent Liabilities

- ____________ liabilities that arise because of events or transactions that have already occurred.
- When potential liabilities meet certain conditions, they must be reported in the financial statements.

Irwin/McGraw-Hill

Contingent Liabilities

Probability of future sacrifice . . .

Amount . . .	Probable	Reasonably Possible	Remote
Can be Estimated			
Cannot be Estimated			

Present and Future Value Concepts

$1,000 invested today at 10%.

In 5 years it will be worth $1,610.51.

In 25 years it will be worth $10,834.71!

Money can grow over time, because it can earn ____________.

Present and Future Value Concepts

The growth is a mathematical function of four variables:

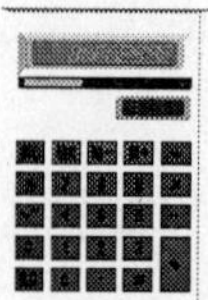

1. The value today.
2. The value in the future.
3. The growth rate, or interest rate.
4. The length of time for growth.

Present and Future Value Concepts

Two types of cash flows can be involved:

Periodic payments called annuities.

Today

Single payment

Present and Future Value Concepts

- **All time value problems are based on the basic interest formula:**

Interest = Principal × Interest Rate × Time

- **Using interest tables makes solving time value problems more efficient.**

Time Value Tables

Tables are available for:

Future value, single amount.

Present value, single amount.

Future value, annuity.

Present value, annuity.

Future Value of a Single Amount

How much will an amount today be worth in the future?

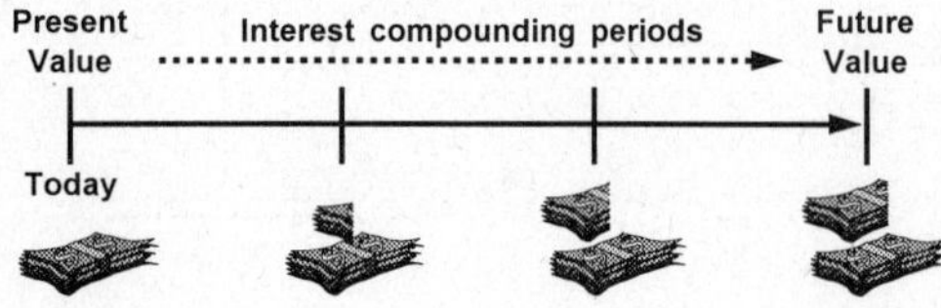

Future Value of a Single Amount

How much will an amount today be worth in the future?

Three pieces of information must be known to answer the question:

❶The current amount.

❷The interest rate (i).

❸The number of periods (n) the amount will be invested.

Future Value of a Single Amount

If we invest $1,000 today earning 10% interest, compounded annually, how much will it be worth in three (3) years?

a. $1,000
b. $1,010
c. $1,100
d. $1,331

Present Value of a Single Amount

How much is a future amount worth today?

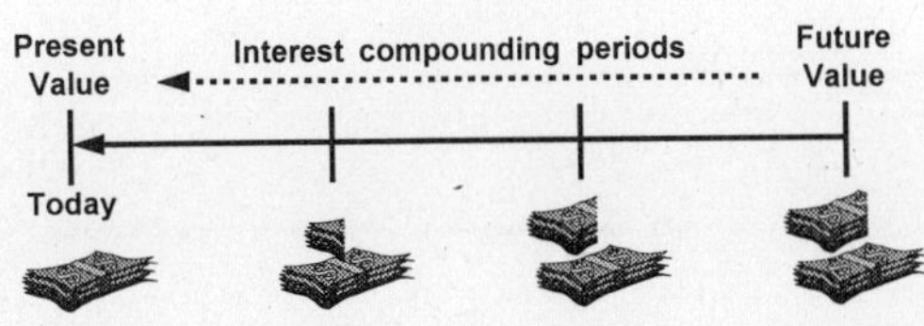

Present Value of a Single Amount

How much is a future amount worth today?

Three pieces of information must be known to solve a present value problem:

- ➊ **The future amount.**
- ➋ **The interest rate (i).**
- ➌ **The number of periods (n) the amount will be invested.**

Present Value of a Single Amount

How much do we need to invest today at 10% interest, compounded annually, if we need $1,331 in three (3) years?

a. **$1,000.00**
b. **$ 990.00**
c. **$ 751.30**
d. **$ 970.00**

Future Value of an Annuity

- Equal payments are made each period.
- The payments and interest accumulate over time.

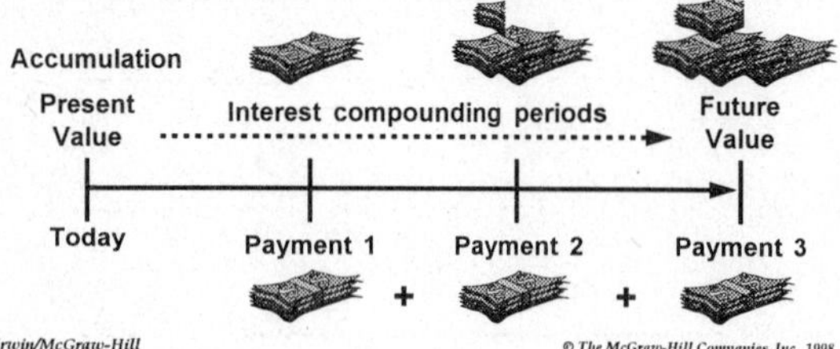

Future Value of an Annuity

If we invest $1,000 each year at interest of 10%, compounded annually, how much will we have at the end of three years?

a. $3,000
b. $3,090
c. $3,300
d. $3,310

Present Value of an Annuity

What is the value today of a series of payments to be received or paid out in the future?

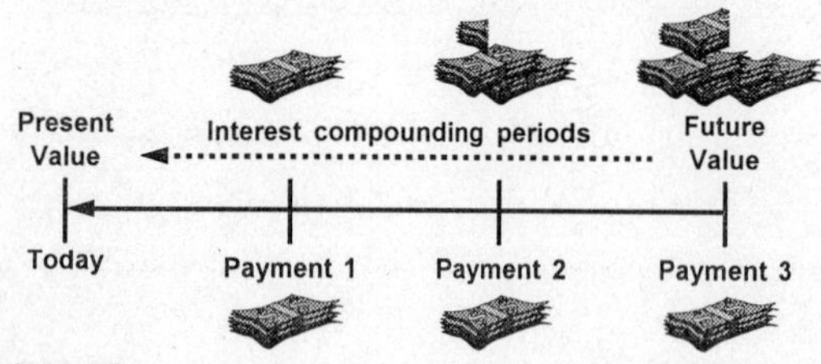

Present Value of an Annuity

What is the present value of receiving $1,000 each year for three years at interest of 10%, compounded annually?

a. $3,000.00
b. $2,910.00
c. $2,700.00
d. $2,486.90

Interest Rates and Interest Periods

When the interest period is for a full year, the interest rate and the number of interest periods are as stated.

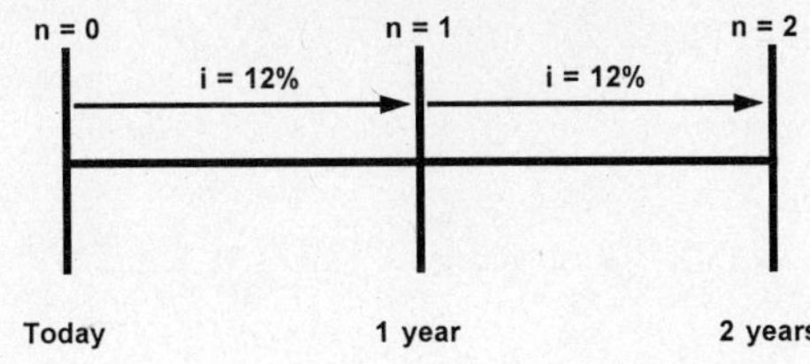

10

REPORTING AND INTERPRETING BONDS

Bonds Payable

At Bond Issuance Date

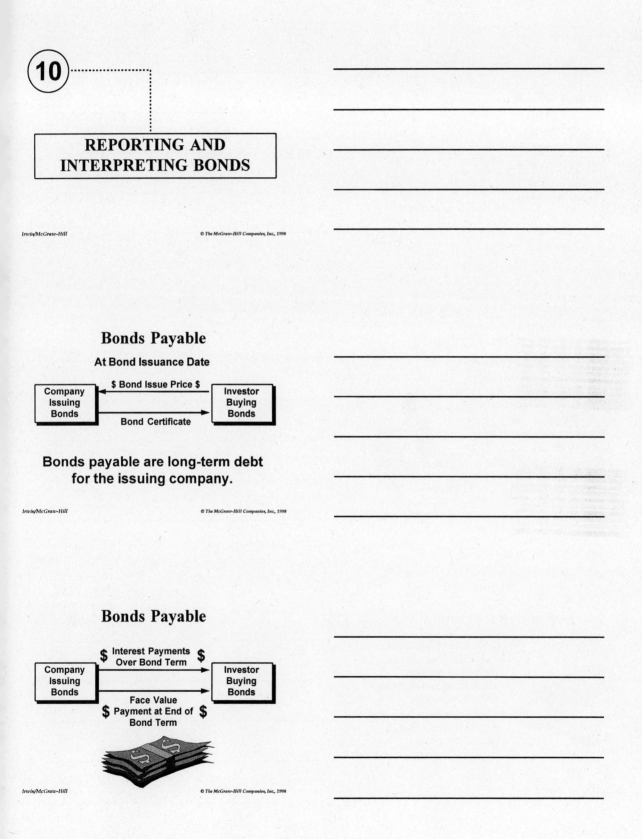

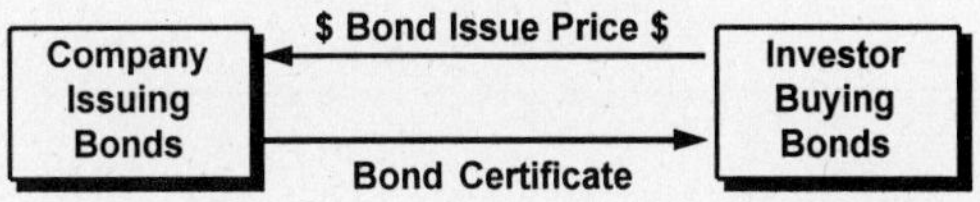

Company Issuing Bonds ← $ Bond Issue Price $ ← Investor Buying Bonds

Company Issuing Bonds → Bond Certificate → Investor Buying Bonds

Bonds payable are long-term debt for the issuing company.

Bonds Payable

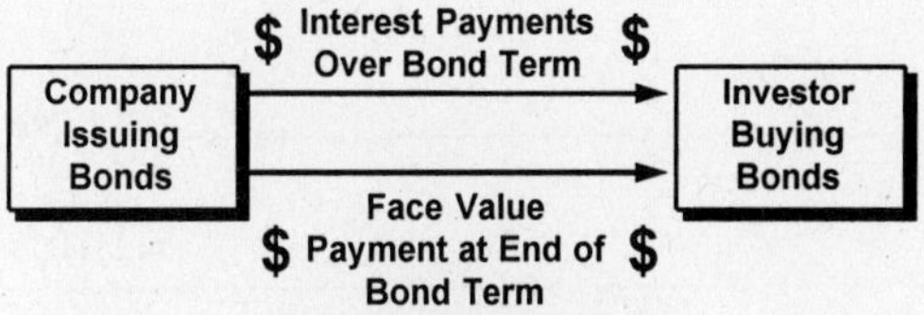

Company Issuing Bonds → $ Interest Payments Over Bond Term $ → Investor Buying Bonds

Company Issuing Bonds → $ Face Value Payment at End of Bond Term $ → Investor Buying Bonds

Business Background

Bonds can be traded on established exchanges that provide liquidity to bondholders.

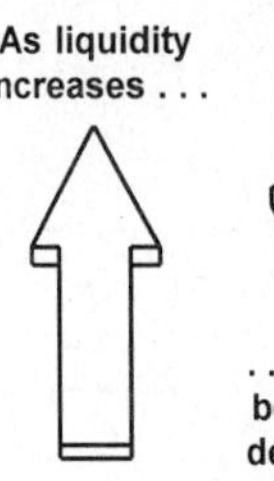

Business Background

Other advantages of bonds:

❶Bonds are debt, not equity, so the ownership and control of the company are not diluted.

❷Interest expense is tax-deductible.

❸The low interest rates on bonds allow for positive financial leverage.

Business Background

Disadvantages of bonds:

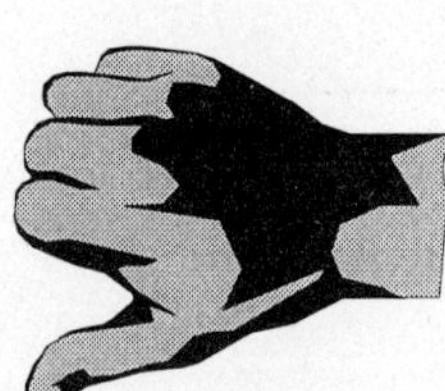

❶The scheduled interest payments are legal obligations and must be paid each period.

❷A single, large principal payment is required at the maturity date.

Financial Analysis

The debt-equity ratio is an important measure of the balance between debt and equity.

$$\text{Debt/equity ratio} = \frac{\text{Total liabilities}}{\text{Owners' equity}}$$

Large debt-equity ratios indicate high leverage and more risk.

Bonds Payable

Face Value $1,000	Interest 10% 6/30 & 12/31
BOND PAYABLE	
Bond Date 1/1/94	Maturity Date 1/1/99

1. Face Value = Maturity or Par Value, Principal
2. Maturity Date
3. Stated Interest Rate
4. Interest Payment Dates
5. Bond Date

Other Factors:

6. Market Interest Rate
7. Issue Date

Characteristics of Bonds Payable

- **When issuing bonds, potential buyers of the bonds are given a prospectus.**
- **The company's bonds are issued to investors through an underwriter.**
- **The trustee makes sure the issuer fulfills all of the provisions of the bond indenture.**

Bond Classifications

- **Callable bonds**
  - ❖May be retired and repaid (called) at any time at the option of the issuer.
- **Redeemable bonds**
  - ❖May be turned in at any time for repayment at the option of the bondholder.
- **Convertible bonds**
  - ❖May be exchanged for other securities of the issuer (usually shares of common stock) at the option of the bondholder.

Bond Classifications

- **Senior Debt receives preference over other creditors in the event of bankruptcy or default.**
- **Subordinated Debt is riskier than senior debt.**

Measuring Bonds Payable and Interest Expense

The issue price of the bond is determined by the market, based on the time value of money.

	Present Value of the Principal (a single payment)
+	Present Value of the Interest Payments (an annuity)
=	Issue Price of the Bond

The interest rate used to compute the present value is the market interest rate.

Measuring Bonds Payable and Interest Expense

The stated rate, or coupon rate, is only used to compute the periodic interest payments.

Interest = Principal × Stated Rate × Time

Bonds Issued at a Discount

Interest Rates	Bond Price	Accounting for the Difference
Stated Rate = Market Rate	Bond Price = Par Value of the Bond	There is no difference to account for.
Stated Rate < Market Rate	Bond Price < Par Value of the Bond	The difference is accounted for as a bond discount.
Stated Rate > Market Rate	Bond Price > Par Value of the Bond	The difference is accounted for as a bond premium.

Issuing Bonds - Example

On May 1, 1999, Repto Corp. issues $1,000,000 in bonds having a stated rate of 6% annually. The bonds mature in 10 years and interest is paid semiannually. The market rate is 8% annually.

Are Repto's bonds issued at par, at a discount, or at a premium?

Issuing Bonds - Example

On May 1, 1999, Repto Corp. issues $1,000,000 in bonds having a stated rate of 6% annually. The bonds mature in 10 years and interest is paid semiannually. The market rate is 8% annually.

Interest Rates	Bond Price	Accounting for the Difference
Stated Rate < Market Rate	Bond Price < Par Value of the Bond	The difference is accounted for as a bond discount.

Issuing Bonds - Example

❶Compute the present value of the principal.

❷Compute the present value of the interest payments.

❸Compute the issue price of the bonds.

Recording Bonds Issued at a Discount

❹Prepare the journal entry to record the issuance of the bonds.

GENERAL JOURNAL Page 97

Date		Description	Post. Ref.	Debit	Credit

Bonds Issued at a Discount
Financial Statement Presentation

Repto Corporation
Partial Balance Sheet
5/1/99

Long-Term Liabilities	
Bonds Payable, 6%	$ 1,000,000
Due April 30, 2009	
Less: Bond Discount	(135,891)
Total L-T Liabilities	$ 864,109

The discount will be amortized over the 10-year life of the bonds.

Straight-Line Amortization of Bond Discount

❶ Identify the amount of the bond discount.

❷ Divide the bond discount by the number of interest periods.

❸ Include the discount amortization amount as part of the periodic interest expense entry.

❖ The discount will be reduced to zero by the maturity date.

Straight-Line Amortization of Bond Discount

Repto Corp. issued their bonds on May 1, 1999. The discount was $135,891. The bonds have a 10-year maturity and $30,000 interest is paid semiannually.

Compute the periodic discount amortization amount using the straight-line method.

Straight-Line Amortization of Bond Discount

Repto Corp. issued their bonds on May 1, 1999. The discount was $135,891. The bonds have a 10-year maturity and $30,000 interest is paid semiannually.

Discount Amortization = Total Discount ÷ Number of Interest Periods

Straight-Line Amortization of Bond Discount

Prepare the journal entry to record the payment of interest and the discount amortization for the six months ending on November 1, 1999.

GENERAL JOURNAL Page 123

Date		Description	Post. Ref.	Debit	Credit

Bonds Issued at a Discount
Financial Statement Presentation

Repto Corporation
Partial Balance Sheet
11/1/99

Long-Term Liabilities	
Bonds Payable, 6%	$ 1,000,000
Due April 30, 2009	
Less: Bond Discount	(129,096)
Total L-T Liabilities	$ 870,904

Note that as the discount is amortized, the carrying amount of the bonds increases.

Zero Coupon Bonds

- Bonds that do not pay periodic interest.
- With no interest . . .

PV of the Principal = Issue Price of the Bonds

- This is called a deep discount bond.

Issuing Bonds - Example

On May 1, 1998, Growler, Inc. issues $1,000,000 in bonds having a stated rate of 10% annually. The bonds mature in 10 years and interest is paid semiannually. The market rate is 8% annually.

Are Growler's bonds issued at par, at a discount, or at a premium?

Issuing Bonds - Example

❶ Compute the present value of the principal.

❷ Compute the present value of the interest payments.

❸ Compute the issue price of the bonds.

Recording Bonds Issued at a Premium

❹ Prepare the journal entry to record the issuance of the bonds.

GENERAL JOURNAL Page 97

Date		Description	Post. Ref.	Debit	Credit

Bonds Issued at a Premium
Financial Statement Presentation

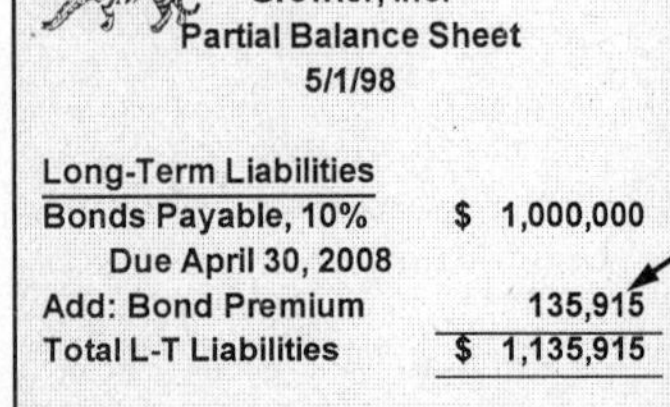

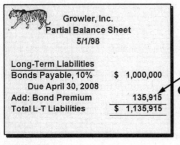

Growler, Inc.
Partial Balance Sheet
5/1/98

Long-Term Liabilities	
Bonds Payable, 10% Due April 30, 2008	$ 1,000,000
Add: Bond Premium	135,915
Total L-T Liabilities	$ 1,135,915

The premium will be amortized over the 10-year life of the bonds.

Straight-Line Amortization of Bond Premium

❶ Identify the amount of the bond premium.

❷ Divide the bond premium by the number of interest periods.

❸ Include the premium amortization amount as part of the periodic interest expense entry.

- ❖ The premium will be reduced to zero by the maturity date.

Straight-Line Amortization of Bond Premium

Growler, Inc. issued their bonds on May 1, 1998. The premium was $135,915. The bonds have a 10-year maturity and $50,000 interest is paid semiannually.

Compute the periodic premium amortization amount using the straight-line method.

Straight-Line Amortization of Bond Premium

Prepare the journal entry to record the payment of interest and the premium amortization for the six months ending on November 1, 1998.

GENERAL JOURNAL Page 123

Date		Description	Post. Ref.	Debit	Credit

Bonds Issued at a Premium
Financial Statement Presentation

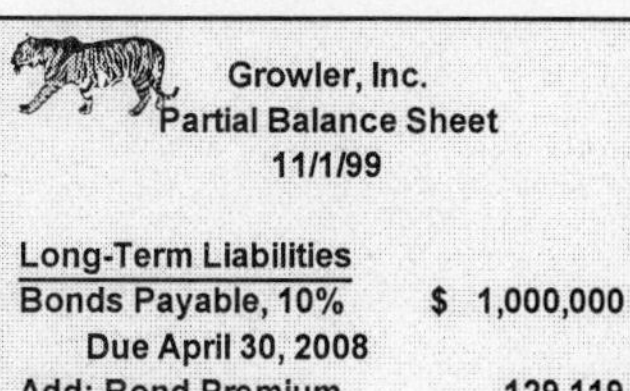

Growler, Inc.
Partial Balance Sheet
11/1/99

Long-Term Liabilities	
Bonds Payable, 10%	$ 1,000,000
Due April 30, 2008	
Add: Bond Premium	129,119
Total L-T Liabilities	$ 1,129,119

Note that as the premium is amortized, the carrying amount of the bonds decreases.

Effective-Interest Amortization of Bond Discounts and Premiums

The effective-interest method computes interest as:

Bond Carrying Value × Market Rate

Effective-Interest Amortization of Bond Discounts and Premiums

The effective-interest method computes interest as:

Bond Carrying Value × Market Rate

The premium or discount amortization amount is the difference between the effective interest expense and the stated interest payment.

Irwin/McGraw-Hill
© The McGraw-Hill Companies, Inc., 1998

Effective-Interest Method

On June 30, 1998, Gusher Corp. issues $100,000 of bonds having a 3-year maturity and a 8% stated annual rate of interest. Interest is paid semiannually. On June 30, the market rate is 10%.

Are Gusher's bonds issued at par, at a discount, or at a premium?

Irwin/McGraw-Hill
© The McGraw-Hill Companies, Inc., 1998

Effective-Interest Method

❶ Compute the present value of the principal.

❷ Compute the present value of the interest payments.

❸ Compute the issue price of the bonds.

Effective-Interest Method

Set up an amortization table for the bonds payable.

Effective-Interest Method Amortization Table

Date	(a) Interest Payment	(b) Interest Expense	(c) Amortization	(d) Carrying Amount
6/30/98				$ 94,923
12/31/98	$ 4,000	$ 4,746	$ 746	95,669
6/30/99	4,000	4,783	783	96,452
12/31/99	4,000	4,823	823	97,275
6/30/00	4,000	4,864	864	98,139
12/31/00	4,000	4,907	907	99,046
6/30/01	4,000	4,954	954	100,000

Understanding Notes to Financial Statements

- Effective-interest method of amortization is preferred by GAAP.
- Straight-line amortization may be used if it is not materially different from effective interest amortization.

Bonds Issued Between Interest Dates

- Bonds are often issued between interest dates.
- The issuing price of the bond is computed as:

	Present value of the bond
+	Accrued interest since the last interest payment
=	Issuing price of the bond

Early Retirement of Debt

- When a bondholder issues a bond, there is no effect on the books of the issuing company.
- Occasionally, the issuing company will call (repay early) some or all of its bonds.
- Gains/losses incurred as a result of retiring bonds, should be reported as an extraordinary item on the income statement.

Bond Sinking Funds

- A special fund to be used to retire bonds at maturity.
- Normally, periodic cash contributions are made to the fund.
- Usually reported on the balance sheet as a noncurrent asset.

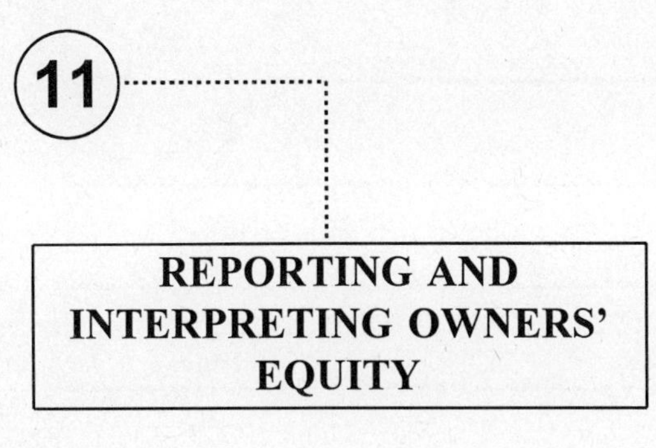

Business Background

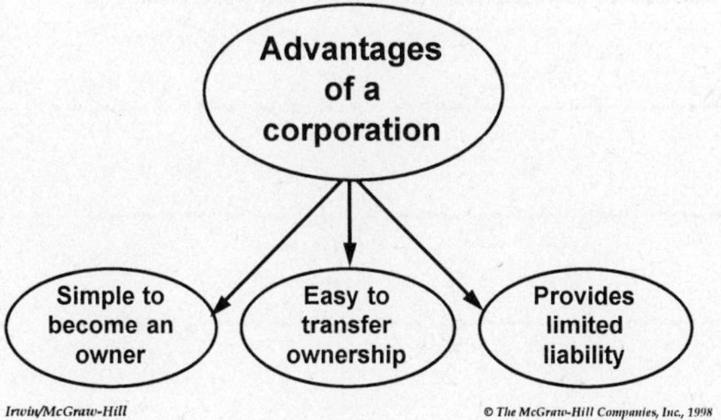

Business Background

Because a corporation is a separate legal entity, it can . . .

- Own assets.
- Incur liabilities.
- Sue and be sued.
- Enter into contracts.

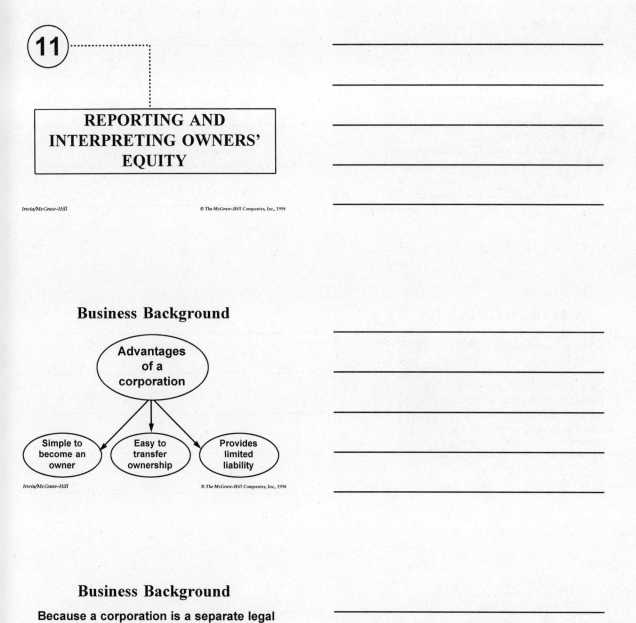

Ownership of a Corporation

Stockholders

Rights

❶Voting (in person or by proxy).

❷Proportionate distributions of profits.

❸Proportionate distributions of assets in a liquidation.

Creating a Corporation

Once the state issues a charter, the stockholders elect a board of directors.

Authorized, Issued, and Outstanding Capital Stock

Authorized Shares

The maximum number of shares of capital stock that can be sold to the public.

Authorized, Issued, and Outstanding Capital Stock

Authorized Shares

Issued shares are authorized shares of stock that have been sold.

Unissued shares are authorized shares of stock that never have been sold.

Authorized, Issued, and Outstanding Capital Stock

Authorized Shares

Outstanding shares are issued shares that are owned by stockholders.

Issued Shares

Outstanding Shares

Unissued Shares

Treasury Shares

Treasury shares are issued shares that have been reacquired by the corporation.

Types of Capital Stock

Common Stock

Preferred Stock

Common Stock

Basic voting stock

Ranks after preferred stock

Dividend set by board of directors

Par Value and No-par Value Stock

Par Value

Nominal value

Legal capital

Legal capital is the amount of capital, required by the state, that must remain invested in the business.

Par Value and No-par Value Stock

Par Value ≠ Market Value

I get it!

Par Value and No-par Value Stock

Some states do not require that a par value be stated in the charter.
No-Par Value
Irwin/McGraw-Hill
© The McGraw-Hill Companies, Inc., 1998

Par Value and No-par Value Stock

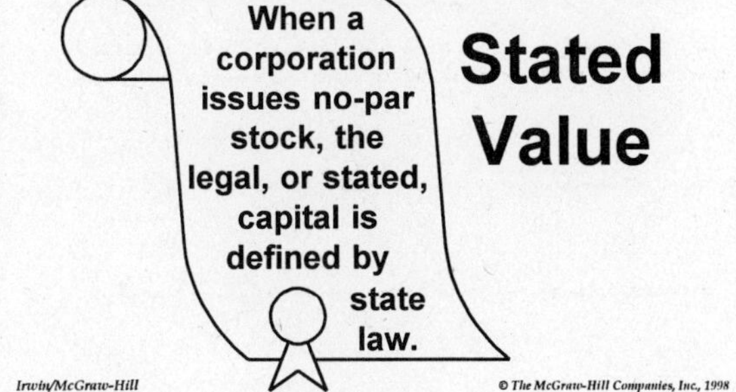

When a corporation issues no-par stock, the legal, or stated, capital is defined by state law.
Stated Value
Irwin/McGraw-Hill
© The McGraw-Hill Companies, Inc., 1998

Preferred Stock

Preference over common stock

Usually has no voting rights

Usually has a fixed dividend rate

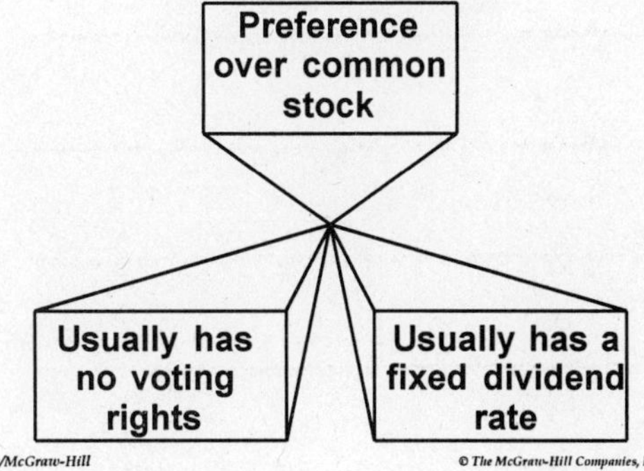

Special Features of Preferred Stock

Convertible preferred stock may be exchanged for common stock.

Callable preferred stock may be repurchased by the corporation at a predetermined price.

Accounting for Capital Stock

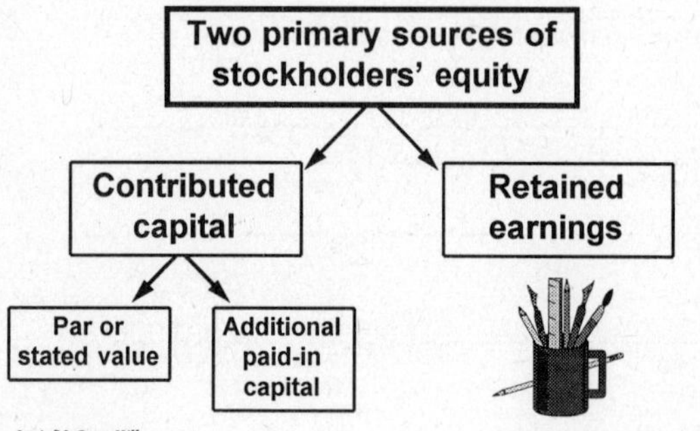

Sale and Issuance of Capital Stock

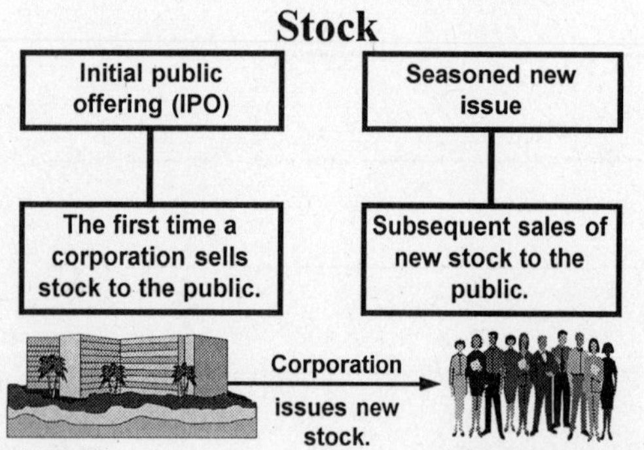

Secondary Markets

Transactions between two investors that do not affect the corporation's accounting records.

Sale and Issuance of Capital Stock

On July 6, East Corp. issued 100,000 shares of $0.10 par value common stock for $25 per share.

Prepare the journal entry to record this transaction.

Page 34

Date		Description	Post. Ref.	Debit	Credit

Capital Stock Sold for Noncash Assets and/or Services

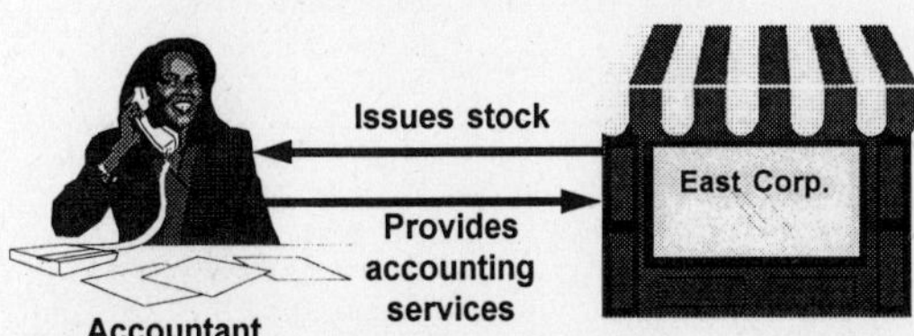

Record assets or services received at the market value of the stock at the date of the transaction.

Capital Stock Sold for Noncash Assets and/or Services

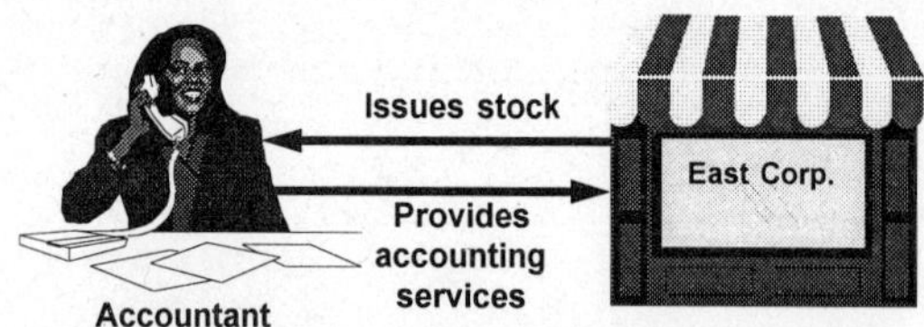

If the market value of the stock cannot be determined, then the market value of the assets or services received should be used.

Capital Stock Sold for Noncash Assets and/or Services

On March 14, East Corp. issued 10,000 shares of its $0.10 par value common stock to King and Associates for legal services. The stock was selling for $25 per share.

Prepare the journal entry to record this transaction.

Date					Credit

Stock Options

If East Corp. does not have new stock to issue when the stock options are exercised, then . .

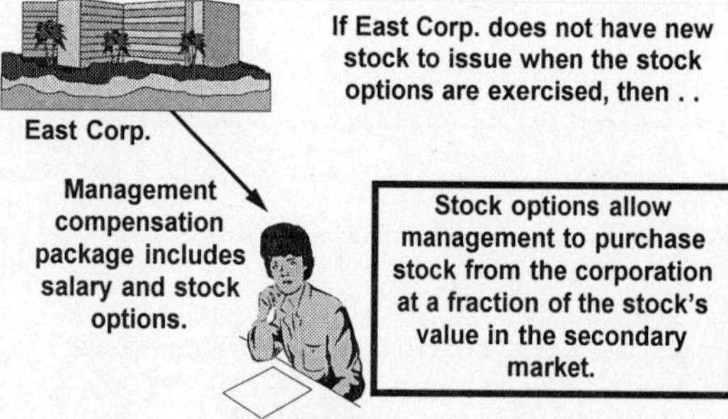

Stock options allow management to purchase stock from the corporation at a fraction of the stock's value in the secondary market.

Stock Options

East Corp. buys its own stock in the secondary market.

Stockholders

East Corp.

Management compensation package includes salary and stock options.

Stock options allow management to purchase stock from the corporation at a fraction of the stock's value in the secondary market.

Management

Treasury Stock

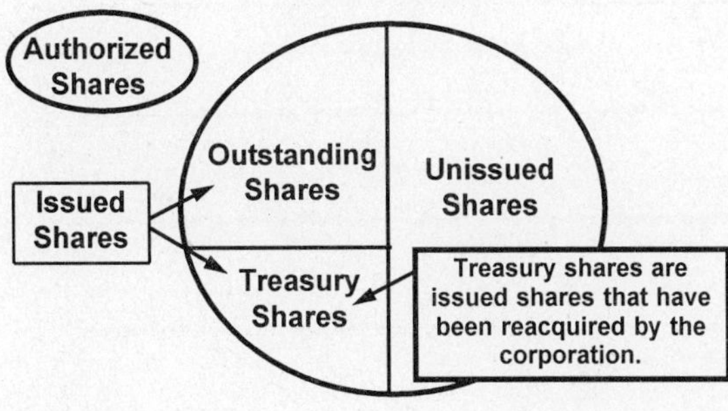

Treasury Stock

No voting or dividend rights

Contra equity account

When stock is reacquired, the corporation records the treasury stock at cost.

Treasury Stock

On May 1, 1998 East Corp. reacquired 3,000 shares of its common stock at $55 per share.

Prepare the journal entry for May 1.

GENERAL JOURNAL — Page 27

Date		Description	Post. Ref.	Debit	Credit

Treasury Stock

On December 3, 1999 East Corp. reissued 1,000 shares of the stock at $75 per share.

Prepare the journal entry for December 3.

GENERAL JOURNAL — Page 68

Date		Description	Post. Ref.	Debit	Credit

Accounting for Cash Dividends

Declared by board of directors.

Not legally required.

Creates liability at declaration.

Requires sufficient Retained Earnings and Cash.

Dividend Dates

- **Declaration date**
  - ❖Board of directors declares the dividend.
  - ❖Record a liability.

GENERAL JOURNAL					Page 12
Date		Description	Post. Ref.	Debit	Credit
		Retained Earnings		XXX	
		Dividends Payable			XXX

Dividend Dates

- **Date of Record**
  - ❖Stockholders holding shares on this date will receive the dividend. **(No entry)**

			1	2	3	4
5	6	7	8	9	10	11
12	13	14	15	16	17	18
19	20	21	22	23	24	25
26	27	28	29	30	31 X	

Dividend Dates

- **Date of Payment**
  - ❖Record the payment of the dividend to stockholders.

GENERAL JOURNAL					Page 12
Date		Description	Post. Ref.	Debit	Credit
		Dividends Payable		XXX	
		Cash			XXX

Dividend Dates
Question

On June 1, 1999 a corporation's board of directors declared a dividend for the 2,500 shares of its $100 par value, 8% preferred stock. The dividend will be paid on July 15. Which of the following will be included in the July 15 entry?

a. Debit Retained Earnings $20,000.
b. Debit Dividends Payable $20,000.
c. Credit Dividends Payable $20,000.
d. Credit Preferred Stock $20,000.

Dividends on Preferred Stock

1. Current Dividend Preference: The current preferred dividends must be paid before paying any dividends to common stock.
2. Cumulative Dividend Preference: Any unpaid dividends from previous years (dividends in arrears) must be paid before common dividends are paid.

Dividends on Preferred Stock

If the preferred stock is noncumulative, any dividends not declared in previous years are lost permanently.

Dividends on Preferred Stock

Kites, Inc. has the following stock outstanding:

Common stock: $1 par, 100,000 shares
Preferred stock: 3%, $100 par, cumulative, 5,000 shares
Preferred stock: 6%, $50 par, noncumulative, 3,000 shares

Dividends were not paid last year. In the current year, the board of directors declared dividends of $50,000.

How much will each class of stock receive?

Dividends on Preferred Stock

Total dividend declared	$ 50,000
Preferred stock (cumulative)	
Arrearage	
Current Yr.	
Remainder	
Preferred stock (noncumulative)	
Current Yr.	
Remainder	
Common stock	
Current Yr.	
Remainder	

Accounting for Stock Dividends

Distribution of additional shares of stock to stockholders.

- No change in total stockholders' equity.
- No change in par values.
- All stockholders retain same percentage ownership.

Small Stock Dividends

Stock dividend < 20% to 25%

↓

Record at current market value of stock.

Irwin/McGraw-Hill

Large Stock Dividends

Stock dividend > 20% to 25%

↓

Record at par or stated value of stock.

Irwin/McGraw-Hill

Stock Splits

Distributions of 100% or more of stock to stockholders.

Ice Cream Parlor

Banana Splits On Sale Now

Irwin/McGraw-Hill

Stock Splits

Assume that a corporation had 5,000 shares of $1 par value common stock outstanding before a 2–for–1 stock split.

	Before Split	After Split
Common Stock Shares	5,000	
Par Value per Share	$ 1.00	
Total Par Value	$ 5,000	

Restrictions on Retained Earnings

Restrictions on Retained Earnings

Restrictions on Retained Earnings

Irwin/McGraw-Hill

Accounting and Reporting for Unincorporated Businesses

	Corporation (Stockholders' Equity)	Sole Proprietorship (Owner's Equity)	Partnership (Partners' Equity)
Equity Accounts	Capital Stock	Doe, Capital	Able, Capital Baker, Capital
	Contributed Capital in Excess of Par	Not used	Not used
	Retained Earnings	Not used	Not used
Distributions to Owners	Dividends Paid	Doe, Drawings	Able, Drawings Baker, Drawings
Closing Entires	Income Summary (closed to Retained Earnings)	Income Summary (closed to Doe, Capital)	Income Summary (closed to Able, Capital and Baker, Capital)
Income Statement	Revenues, expenses, gains and losses	Same	Same
Balance Sheet	Assets and liabilities	Same	Same

Irwin/McGraw-Hill

End of Chapter 11

Irwin/McGraw-Hill

12

REPORTING AND INTERPRETING INVESTMENTS IN OTHER CORPORATIONS

Business Background

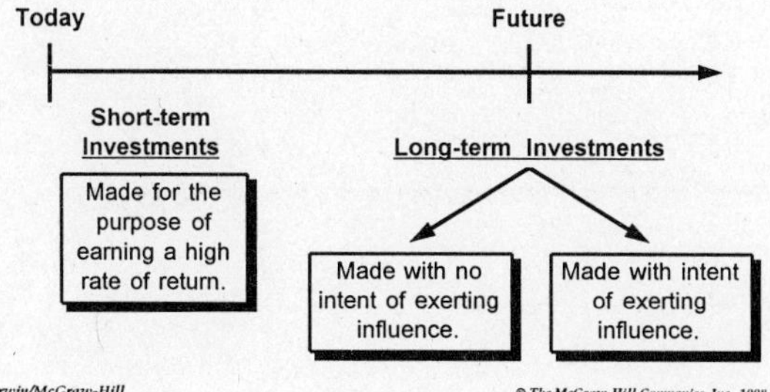
Today
Future
Short-term Investments
Made for the purpose of earning a high rate of return.
Long-term Investments
Made with no intent of exerting influence.
Made with intent of exerting influence.

Business Background

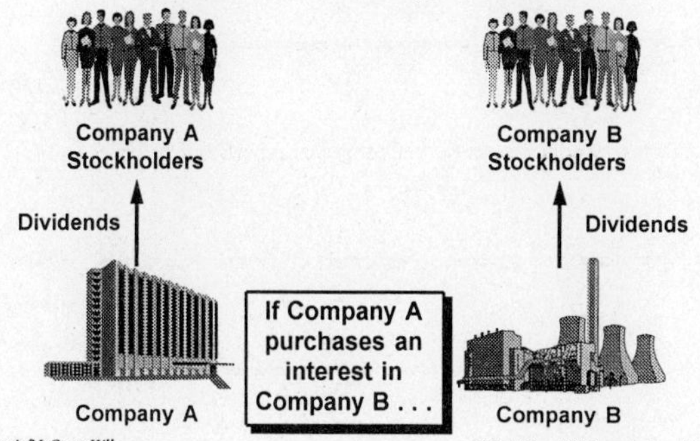
Company A Stockholders
Company B Stockholders
Dividends
Dividends
If Company A purchases an interest in Company B . . .
Company A
Company B

Accounting for Investments in Securities

The degree of influence and control a company has affects how the investment is accounted for.

Level of Influence	Accounting Method
No influence or control	Market value method
Significant influence, but no control	Equity method
Control	Consolidated statement method

Market Value Method

Used when less than 20% of the outstanding voting stock is held.

Level of Influence	Accounting Method
No influence or control	Market value method
Significant influence, but no control	Equity method
Control	Consolidated statement method

Market Value Method

Date of acquisition

Unrealized holding gains and losses are recognized.

Future measurement date

Investment is initially recorded at cost.

Investment carrying amount is adjusted to current market value.

Market Value Method

Type of Investment	Definition	Effect of Unrealized Holding Gains and Losses On . . .		
		Investment Account	Equity	Net Income
Trading Securities	Held primarily for resale.	Allowance Account	N/A	Reported on the Income Statement
Available-for-Sale Securities	Not held primarily for resale.	Allowance Account	Reported as part of equity	N/A

NOTE: Realized gains and losses appear on the Income Statement.

Market Value Method

Unrealized holding gains and losses from trading securities are reported on the income statement.

Big Company
Partial Income Statement
For the Year Ended 12/31/99

Income from operations	$ 3,000
Unrealized holding loss	(8,000)
Net loss	$ (5,000)

Market Value Method

Big Company
Partial Balance Sheet
12/31/99

Stockholders' Equity	
Common stock	$ 50,000
Paid-in-capital	125,000
Unrealized holding loss	(8,000)
Retained Earnings	27,000
Total Stockholders' Equity	$ 194,000

Unrealized holding gains and losses from available-for-sale securities are reported in the equity section of the balance sheet.

Market Value Method Example

Images, Inc. and Castle Productions, Inc. both produce films. Castle wants to acquire an ownership interest in Images.

On 6/30/98, Castle acquires 2% of Images' 1,000,000 shares on the open market at a cost of $18 per share. Castle has no influence over Images, and does not plan to sell the shares in the near future.

Market Value Method Example

Should Castle's shares be classified as Trading Securities or Available-for-Sale Securities?

Market Value Method Example

By December 31, 1998, Castle's fiscal year-end, the market value of Images' shares has dropped to $16 per share.

How much has Castle's portfolio value changed?

Selling Trading Securities

Effects	Trading Securities	Available-for-Sale Securities
Income Statement		
Realized Gains	Sales Price > Cost	Same
Realized Losses	Sales Price < Cost	Same
Unrealized Gains and Losses	Adjust at Year-end	N/A
Balance Sheet		
Unrealized Gains and Losses	N/A	Adjust at Year-end

Equity Method

Used when an investor can exert significant influence over an investee.

Level of Influence	Accounting Method
No influence or control	Market value method
Significant influence, but no control	Equity method
Control	Consolidated statement method

It is presumed that the investment was made as a long-term investment.

Equity Method

Date of acquisition

Unrealized holding gains and losses are not recognized.

Future measurement date

Investment is initially recorded at cost.

Investment carrying amount is adjusted for dividends received from the investee, a % share of the income of the investee, and amortization of goodwill.

Equity Method

Adjusting Item	Effect on Investment Account
Dividends	Reduce investment for dividends received.
Investee Net Income	Increase investment by our proportionate share.
Investee Net Loss	Decrease investment by our proportionate share.

Equity Method Example

On 1/1/99, The Super Network (TSN) acquires a 30% interest in Sports Films, Inc. at a cost of $2,000,000. Prepare the journal entry to record TSN's investment.

TSN's General Journal Page 2

Date		Description	PR	Debit	Credit

Equity Method Example

On 3/31/99, Sports Films pays $200,000 in dividends, $60,000 of which goes to TSN. Record TSN's receipt of the dividend.

TSN's General Journal Page 46

Date		Description	PR	Debit	Credit

Equity Method Example

Sports Films' net income for the year ending 12/31/99 is $1,600,000. TSN's 30% share is $480,000. Record the appropriate journal entry on TSN's books at 12/31/99.

GENERAL JOURNAL Page 144

Date		Description	PR	Debit	Credit

Achieving Control

Clearing the 20% hurdle to gain influence . . .

Vaulting over the 50% mark to gain control!

Off and running with less than 20% . . .

Investing to Achieve a Controlling Interest

- Horizontal integration
- Synergy
- Vertical integration
- Diversification
- Special assets
- Undervalued opportunities

Investing to Achieve a Controlling Interest

- The acquiring company is the parent.
- The acquired company is the subsidiary.
- Consolidated financial statements must be prepared.

Consolidated Financial Statements

- Statements that report the financial information from two or more different companies as if they were one company.
- Intercompany transactions are not reported.

Methods of Acquiring a Controlling Interest

A pooling of interests occurs when two or more companies merge to form a new company.

BANK
Merge
Merge
BANK
Bank A
Bank B
New Great Big Bank

Methods of Acquiring a Controlling Interest

A purchase occurs when one company acquires the voting shares of another company.

Bank A

Bank B

Bank A purchases Bank B.

Goodwill

- **The excess of the purchase price of a company over the fair market value (FMV) of the net assets.**
- **Created by:**
  - ❖Good reputation.
  - ❖Customer appeal and loyalty.
- **Goodwill is only recorded in a purchase transaction.**

Goodwill Example

On 1/1/99, Watch Corp. acquired 100% of the voting stock of Iowa Springs, Inc. for $6,200,000 cash. At the time, Iowa Springs' net assets had an FMV of $6,000,000.

Compute the goodwill acquired by Watch Corp. in this purchase.

13

STATEMENT OF CASH FLOWS

Business Background

Positive cash flows permit a company to . . .

- Pay dividends to owners.
- Expand its operations.
- Take advantage of market opportunities.
- Replace needed assets.

Wall Street analysts consider cash flow an important indicator of a company's financial health.

Classifications on the Statement of Cash Flows (SCF)

Cash

Currency

Cash Equivalents

Categories of Cash Flows

The SCF must include the following three sections:

❶Operating Activities
❷Investing Activities
❸Financing Activities

Cash Flows from Operating Activities

- **Cash inflows and outflows related to selling goods or performing services.**
- **Can be computed using either the direct method or the indirect method.**

Cash Flows from Operating Activities - Direct Method

Inflows include:
- ❖ Receipts from customers.
- ❖ Interest on receivables.
- ❖ Dividends received.

Outflows include:
- ❖ Payments to suppliers.
- ❖ Interest paid on liabilities.
- ❖ Income taxes paid.
- ❖ Salary and wage payments to employees.

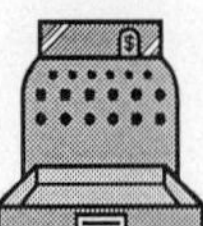

Cash Flows from Operating Activities - Indirect Method

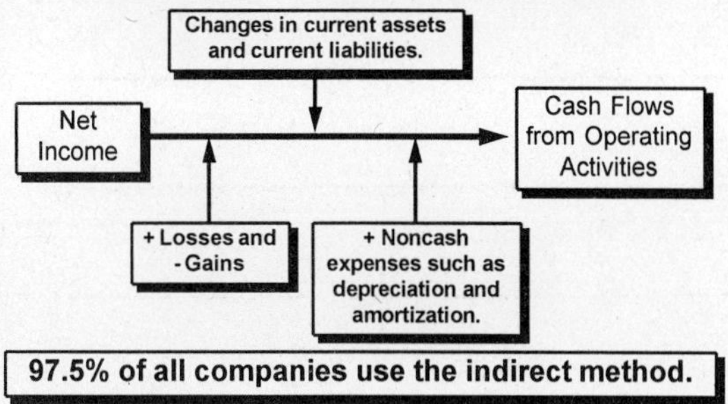

97.5% of all companies use the indirect method.

Cash Flows from Investing Activities

Proceeds from:
- Sales of property, plant, and equipment.
- Sales of investments.
- Collection of principal on loans.

\+

Cash paid to:
- Purchase PP&E.
- Purchase long-term. investments.
- Make loans.

–

Cash Flows from Investing Activities

Cash Flows from Financing Activities

Proceeds from:
- Issuing stock.
- Issuing bonds.
- Borrowings.

\+

Cash paid to:
- Purchase treasury stock.
- Retire bonds.
- Repay loan principal.
- Pay dividends to stockholders.

–

Cash Flows from Financing Activities

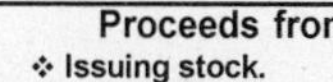

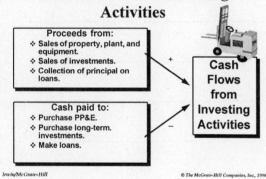

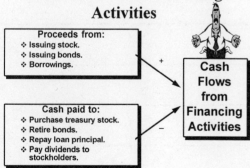

Links to the Balance Sheet and the Income Statement

Information needed to prepare a statement of cash flows:

- **Comparative Balance Sheets.**
- **Income Statement.**
- **Additional details concerning different types of transactions and events.**

Understanding the Cash Flow Statement

Δ Cash = Δ Liabilities + Δ Stockholders' Equity − Δ Noncash Assets

Derives from . . .

Assets = Liabilities + Stockholders' Equity

Understanding the Cash Flow Statement

The face of the statement includes:

	Net Cash Flows from Operating Activities
+	Net Cash Flows from Investing Activities
+	Net Cash Flows from Financing Activities
=	Net Cash Flows for the Period
+	Beginning of Period Cash Balance
=	End of Period Cash Balance

Reporting and Interpreting Cash Flows from Operating Activities

	Change in Account Balance During Year	
	Increase	Decrease
Current Assets	Subtract from net income.	Add to net income.
Current Liabilities	Add to net income.	Subtract from net income.

Use this table when adjusting Net Income to Operating Cash Flows.

Comprehensive SCF Example Using the Indirect Method

Joe's Place has prepared the Balance Sheet as of 3/31/98 and 3/31/97. The Income Statement for the year ended 3/31/98 has also been prepared. Joe needs help preparing the Statement of Cash Flows.

Comprehensive SCF Example Using the Indirect Method

Joe's Place
Income Statement
For the Year Ending 3/31/98

Revenues	$727,000
Operating Expenses	(748,000)
Depreciation Expense	(6,000)
Gain on Sale of Land	8,000
Net Loss	$ (19,000)

Comprehensive SCF Example Using the Indirect Method

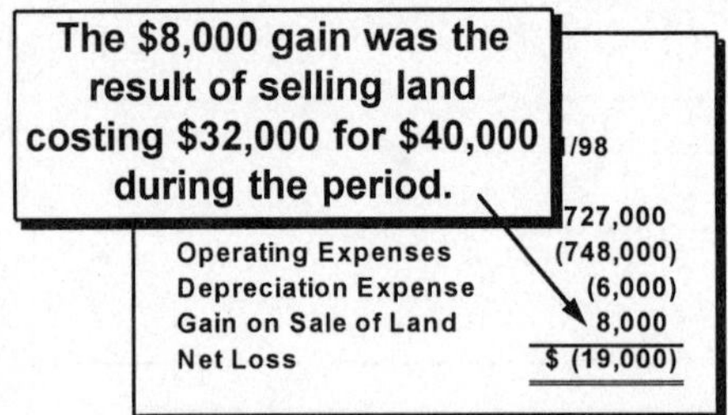

The $8,000 gain was the result of selling land costing $32,000 for $40,000 during the period.
/98
727,000
Operating Expenses (748,000)
Depreciation Expense (6,000)
Gain on Sale of Land 8,000
Net Loss $ (19,000)

Irwin/McGraw-Hill

Comprehensive SCF Example Using the Indirect Method

Joe's Place
Balance Sheets

	3/31/97	3/31/98
Assets		
Cash	$ 90,000	$ 62,000
Accounts Receivable	40,000	23,000
Inventory	300,000	350,000
Land	112,000	80,000
Equipment, net	45,000	39,000
Total Assets	$ 587,000	$ 554,000

Irwin/McGraw-Hill

Comprehensive SCF Example Using the Indirect Method

Joe's Place
Balance Sheets (cont.)

	3/31/97	3/31/98
Liabilities		
Accounts Payable	$ 27,000	$ 38,000
Salaries Payable	14,000	9,000
Long-Term Note Payable	50,000	-
Total Liabilities	$ 91,000	$ 47,000
Owners' Equity		
Common Stock	$ 450,000	$ 500,000
Retained Earnings	46,000	7,000
Total Owners' Equity	$ 496,000	$ 507,000
Total Liabilities and OE	$ 587,000	$ 554,000

Irwin/McGraw-Hill

Comprehensive SCF Example Using the Indirect Method

Joe's Place issued $50,000 of nopar common stock to settle the $50,000 note payable.

	ce s (cont.) 3/31/97	3/31/98
	27,000	$ 38,000
	14,000	9,000
Long-Term Note Payable	50,000	-
Total Liabilities	$ 91,000	$ 47,000
Owners' Equity		
Common Stock	$ 450,000	$ 500,000
Retained Earnings	46,000	7,000
Total Owners' Equity	$ 496,000	$ 507,000
Total Liabilities and OE	$ 587,000	$ 554,000

Comprehensive SCF Example Using the Indirect Method

Ending Retained Earnings at 3/31/98 was computed as follows:

	Beginning R/E, 3/31/97	$ 46,000
–	Net Loss for 1998	(19,000)
–	Dividends Paid in 1998	(20,000)
=	Ending R/E, 3/31/98	$ 7,000

		3/31/98
		$ 38,000
		9,000
		-
		$ 47,000
		$ 500,000
Retained Earnings	46,000	7,000
Total Owners' Equity	$ 496,000	$ 507,000
Total Liabilities and OE	$ 587,000	$ 554,000

Summary of Differences Between Direct and Indirect Methods

- **The direct method provides more detail about cash from operating activities.**
  - ❖Shows individual operating cash flows.
  - ❖Shows reconciliation of operating cash flows to net income in a supplemental schedule.
- **The investing and financing sections for the two methods are identical.**
- **Net cash flow is the same for both methods.**

14

Analyzing Financial Statements

Business Background

FINANCIAL STATEMENT USERS

MANAGEMENT

. . . uses accounting data to make product pricing and expansion decisions.

EXTERNAL DECISION MAKERS

. . . use accounting data for invesment, credit, tax, and public policy decisions.

Business Background

THREE TYPES OF FINANCIAL STATEMENT INFORMATION

Past Performance

Income, sales volume, cash flows, return-on-investments, EPS.

Present Condition

Assets, debt, inventory, various ratios.

Future Performance

Sales and earnings trends are good indicators of future performance.

Business Background

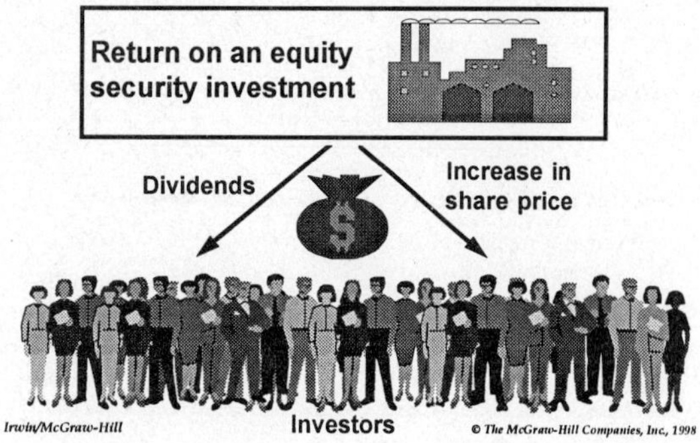

Return on an equity security investment

Dividends

Increase in share price

Investors

Irwin/McGraw-Hill

Business Background

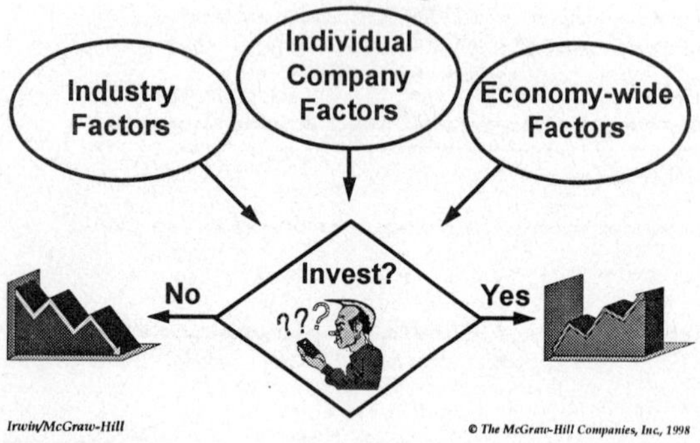

Industry Factors

Individual Company Factors

Economy-wide Factors

Invest?

No

Yes

Irwin/McGraw-Hill

Understanding a Company's Strategy

Financial statement analysis will be more meaningful once I learn more about the company's business strategy from reading the annual report and articles in the business press.

Irwin/McGraw-Hill

Financial Statement Analysis

Financial statement analysis is based on comparisons.

Time series analysis

Comparison with similar companies

Financial Statement Analysis

Financial statement analysis is based on comparisons.

Time series analysis

Examines a single company to identify trends over time.

Comparison with similar companies

Financial Statement Analysis

Financial statement analysis is based on comparisons.

Time series analysis

Company A

Company B

Comparison with similar companies

Provides insights concerning a company's relative performance.

Ratio and Percentage Analyses

Ratio analysis, or percentage analysis, is used to express the proportionate relationship between two different amounts.

%

Component Percentages

Express each item on a particular statement as a percentage of a single base amount.

Net sales on the income statement

Total assets on the balance sheet

Component Percentages

Example

The comparative income statements of Clover Corporation for 1999 and 1998 appear on the next slide.

Prepare component percentage income statements where net sales equal 100%.

Component Percentages

CLOVER CORPORATION Comparative Income Statements For the Years Ended December 31, 1999 and 1998				
	1999	Percent	1998	Percent
Net Sales	$494,000	100.00%	$450,000	100.00%
Cost of merchandise sold	140,000	28.34%	127,000	28.22%
Gross profit	$354,000	71.66%	$323,000	71.78%
Operating expenses	270,000	54.66%	249,000	55.33%
Income from operations	$ 84,000	17.00%	$ 74,000	16.45%
Other expense	4,000	0.81%	4,000	0.89%
Income before income tax	$ 80,000	16.19%	$ 70,000	15.56%
Income tax expense (20%)	16,000	3.24%	14,000	3.11%
Net income	$ 64,000	12.95%	$ 56,000	12.45%

Now, let's
look at some
commonly
used ratios.

Commonly Used Ratios

The 1999 and 1998 income statements and balance sheets for Clover Corporation are presented next.

We will be referring to these financial statements throughout the ratio analyses.

Comparative Statements

CLOVER CORPORATION Comparative Income Statements For the Years Ended December 31, 1999 and 1998	1999	1998
Revenue		
Net sales	$494,000	$450,000
Cost of merchandise sold	140,000	127,000
Gross profit	354,000	323,000
Operating expenses	270,000	249,000
Income from operations	84,000	74,000
Interest expense	2,640	3,200
Other expenses	1,360	800
Income before income tax	80,000	70,000
Income tax expense (20%)	16,000	14,000
Net Income	$ 64,000	$ 56,000

Comparative Statements

CLOVER CORPORATION Comparative Balance Sheets December 31, 1999 and 1998	1999	1998
Assets		
Cash	$ 30,000	$ 20,000
Accounts receivable	20,000	17,000
Merchandise inventory	12,000	10,000
Equipment	60,000	60,000
Less Accumulated depreciation	(15,000)	(12,000)
Building	100,000	100,000
Less Accumulated depreciation	(25,000)	(20,000)
Land	168,000	125,000
Total Assets	$ 350,000	$ 300,000

Continued

Comparative Statements

CLOVER CORPORATION Comparative Balance Sheets, Continued December 31, 1999 and 1998	1999	1998
Liabilities		
Accounts payable	$ 39,000	$ 40,000
Notes payable	33,000	40,000
Total Liabilities	$ 72,000	$ 80,000
Stockholders' Equity		
Common stock, $1 par	$ 27,400	$ 17,000
Paid-in capital	198,100	153,000
Retained earnings	52,500	50,000
Total Stockholders' Equity	278,000	220,000
Total Liabilities & Stockholders' Equity	$350,000	$300,000

Tests of Profitability

Profitability is a primary measure of the overall success of a company.

Now, let's look at the profitability ratios for Clover Corporation for 1999.

Return on Owners' Investment

$$\text{Return on Owners' Investment} = \frac{\text{Income}}{\text{Average Owners' Equity}}$$

$$\text{Return on Owners' Investment} = \frac{\$64{,}000}{(\$278{,}000 + \$220{,}000) \div 2} = 25.70\%$$

This measure indicates how much income was earned for every dollar invested by the owners.

Return on Total Investment

$$\text{Return on Total Investment} = \frac{\text{Income + Interest Expense (net of tax)}}{\text{Average Total Assets}}$$

$$\text{Return on Total Investment} = \frac{\$64{,}000 + (\$2{,}640 \times 0.8)}{(\$350{,}000 + \$300{,}000) \div 2} = 20.34\%$$

This ratio is generally considered the best overall measure of a company's profitability.

Financial Leverage

$$\text{Financial Leverage} = \text{Return on Owners' Investment} - \text{Return on Total Investment}$$

$$\text{Financial Leverage} = 25.70\% - 20.34\% = 5.36\%$$

Financial leverage is the advantage or disadvantage that occurs as the result of earning a return on owners' investment that is different from the return on total investment.

Irwin/McGraw-Hill

Earnings per Share (EPS)

$$\text{EPS} = \frac{\text{Income}}{\text{Average Number of Shares of Common Stock Outstanding}}$$

$$\text{EPS} = \frac{\$64{,}000}{(27{,}400 + 17{,}000) \div 2} = \$2.88$$

Earnings per share is probably the single most widely watched financial ratio.

Irwin/McGraw-Hill

Quality of Income

$$\text{Quality of Income} = \frac{\text{Cash Flow from Operating Activities}}{\text{Net Income}}$$

Cash Flow from Operating Activities

Net Income		$ 64,000
Add	Depreciation	8,000
Deduct	Accounts Receivable Increase	(3,000)
	Inventory Increase	(2,000)
	Accounts Payable Decrease	(1,000)
Cash Flow from Operating Activities		$ 66,000

Irwin/McGraw-Hill

Quality of Income

$$\text{Quality of Income} = \frac{\text{Cash Flow from Operating Activities}}{\text{Net Income}}$$

$$\text{Quality of Income} = \frac{\$66,000}{\$64,000} = 1.031$$

A ratio higher than 1 is considered to indicate higher-quality earnings.

Profit Margin

$$\text{Profit Margin} = \frac{\text{Income (before extraordinary items)}}{\text{Net Sales}}$$

$$\text{Profit Margin} = \frac{\$64,000}{\$494,000} = 12.96\%$$

This ratio describes a company's ability to earn income from sales.

Fixed Asset Turnover Ratio

$$\text{Fixed Asset Turnover} = \frac{\text{Net Sales Revenue}}{\text{Average Net Fixed Assets}}$$

$$\text{Fixed Asset Turnover} = \frac{\$494,000}{(\$288,000 + \$253,000) \div 2} = 1.826$$

This ratio measures a company's ability to generate sales given an investment in fixed assets.

Tests of Liquidity

Tests of liquidity focus on the relationship between current assets and current liabilities.

Now, let's look at the liquidity ratios for Clover Corporation for 1999.

Cash Ratio

$$\text{Cash Ratio} = \frac{\text{Cash + Cash Equivalents}}{\text{Current Liabilities}}$$

$$\text{Cash Ratio} = \frac{\$30,000}{\$39,000} = 0.769 : 1$$

This ratio measures the adequacy of available cash.

Current Ratio

$$\text{Current Ratio} = \frac{\text{Current Assets}}{\text{Current Liabilities}}$$

$$\text{Current Ratio} = \frac{\$62,000}{\$39,000} = 1.59 : 1$$

This ratio measures the ability of the company to pay current debts as they become due.

Quick Ratio (Acid Test)

$$\text{Quick Ratio} = \frac{\text{Quick Assets}}{\text{Current Liabilities}}$$

$$\text{Quick Ratio} = \frac{\$50,000}{\$39,000} = 1.28 : 1$$

This ratio is like the current ratio but measures the company's immediate ability to pay debts.

Receivable Turnover

$$\text{Receivable Turnover} = \frac{\text{Net Credit Sales}}{\text{Average Net Trade Receivables}}$$

$$\text{Receivable Turnover} = \frac{\$494,000}{(\$20,000 + \$17,000) \div 2} = 26.70 \text{ times}$$

This ratio measures how quickly a company collects its accounts receivable.

Average Age of Receivables

$$\text{Average Age of Receivables} = \frac{\text{Days in Year}}{\text{Receivable Turnover}}$$

$$\text{Average Age of Receivables} = \frac{365}{26.70} = 13.67 \text{ days}$$

This ratio measures the average number of days it takes to collect receivables.

Inventory Turnover

$$\text{Inventory Turnover} = \frac{\text{Cost of Goods Sold}}{\text{Average Inventory}}$$

$$\text{Inventory Turnover} = \frac{\$140{,}000}{(\$12{,}000 + \$10{,}000) \div 2} = 12.73 \text{ times}$$

This ratio measures how quickly the company sells its inventory.

Average Days' Supply in Inventory

$$\text{Average Days' Supply in Inventory} = \frac{\text{Days in Year}}{\text{Inventory Turnover}}$$

$$\text{Average Days' Supply in Inventory} = \frac{365}{12.73} = 28.67 \text{ days}$$

This ratio measures the average number of days it takes to sell the inventory.

Tests of Solvency and Equity Position

Tests of solvency measure a company's ability to meet its obligations.

Now, let's look at the solvency ratios for Clover Corporation for 1999.

Times Interest Earned

$$\text{Times Interest Earned} = \frac{\text{Net Income} + \text{Interest Expense} + \text{Income Tax Expense}}{\text{Interest Expense}}$$

$$\text{Times Interest Earned} = \frac{\$64{,}000 + \$2{,}640 + \$16{,}000}{\$2{,}640} = 31.30$$

This ratio indicates a margin of protection for creditors.

Cash Coverage

$$\text{Cash Coverage} = \frac{\text{Cash Flow from Operating Activities Before Interest and Taxes}}{\text{Interest Paid}}$$

Cash Flow from Operating Activities

Net Income		$ 64,000
Add	Depreciation	8,000
Deduct	Accounts Receivable Increase	(3,000)
	Inventory Increase	(2,000)
	Accounts Payable Decrease	(1,000)
Cash Flow from Operating Activities		$ 66,000

Cash Coverage

$$\text{Cash Coverage} = \frac{\text{Cash Flow from Operating Activities Before Interest and Taxes}}{\text{Interest Paid}}$$

$$\text{Cash Coverage} = \frac{\$66{,}000 + \$2{,}640 + \$16{,}000}{\$2{,}640} = 32.06$$

This ratio compares the cash generated with the cash obligations of the period.

Debt/Equity Ratio

$$\text{Debt/Equity Ratio} = \frac{\text{Total Liabilities}}{\text{Owners' Equity}}$$

$$\text{Debt/Equity Ratio} = \frac{\$72{,}000}{\$278{,}000} = .259 : 1$$

This ratio measures the amount of liabilities that exists for each $1 invested by the owners.

Market Tests

Market tests relate the current market price of a share of stock to an indicator of the return that might accrue to the investor.

Now, let's look at the market tests for Clover Corporation for 1999.

Price/Earnings (P/E) Ratio

$$\text{P/E Ratio} = \frac{\text{Current Market Price Per Share}}{\text{Earnings Per Share}}$$

The 12/31/99 market price of Clover Corporation's stock was $73 per share.

This ratio measures the relationship between the current market price of the stock and its earnings per share.

Price/Earnings (P/E) Ratio

$$\text{P/E Ratio} = \frac{\text{Current Market Price Per Share}}{\text{Earnings Per Share}}$$

$$\text{P/E Ratio} = \frac{\$73.00}{\$2.88} = 25.34$$

This ratio measures the relationship between the current market price of the stock and its earnings per share.

Dividend Yield Ratio

$$\text{Dividend Yield} = \frac{\text{Dividends Per Share}}{\text{Market Price Per Share}}$$

The 1999 annual dividend per share for Clover Corporation's common stock is $2.50 per share.

This ratio is often used to compare the dividend-paying performance of different investment alternatives.

Dividend Yield Ratio

$$\text{Dividend Yield} = \frac{\text{Dividends Per Share}}{\text{Market Price Per Share}}$$

$$\text{Dividend Yield} = \frac{\$2.50}{\$73.00} = 3.42\%$$

This ratio is often used to compare the dividend-paying performance of different investment alternatives.

Miscellaneous Ratios

Financial analysts may calculate many other financial ratios to help evaluate and compare investment opportunities.

Now, let's look at book value per share as an example of such a ratio for Clover Corporation for 1999.

Book Value per Share

$$\text{Book Value per Share} = \frac{\text{Common Stock Equity}}{\text{Number of Shares of Common Stock Outstanding}}$$

$$\text{Book Value per Share} = \frac{\$278{,}000}{27{,}400} = \$10.15$$

Book value per share measures the owners' equity in terms of common stock outstanding. Book value per share has no relationship to market value.

Other Analytical Considerations

In addition to financial ratios, special factors might affect company analysis:

- Rapid growth.
- Uneconomical expansion.
- Subjective factors.

Interpreting Ratios

To interpret a ratio, it should be compared with some standard that represents an optimal or desired value.

Ratios may vary because of the company's industry characteristics, nature of operations, size, and accounting policies.

Efficient Markets

A securities market in which prices fully reflect available information is called an efficient market.

In an efficient market, a company's stock reacts quickly when new, relevant information is released about the company.

FAST

Late Breaking News

End of Chapter 14

Ratios

Ratios

Ratios

Ratios

Ratios